Mysterious & Unknown Belgium

Cois Geysen

Mysterious & Unknow Belgium

Ley lines and places of power

Uitgeverij Aspekt

Mysterious & Unknown Belgium
© Cois Geysen
© 2013 Uitgeverij ASPEKT
Amersfoortsestraat 27, 3769 AD Soesterberg, Nederland
info@uitgeverijaspekt.nl – http://www.uitgeverijaspekt.nl
Omslagontwerp: Mark Heuveling
Binnenwerk: Paul Timmerman, Amersfoort

ISBN-13: 978-94-6153-329-6
NUR: 680

All rights reserved. No reproduction copy or transmission of this publication may be made without written permission.

Contents

Introduction	7
Ley lines	9
Dowsing	
The power of the places	14
Saints at the right place	15
Miraculous healings	19
Bad athmosphere	20
Dragons and green men	21
Flanders	25
Province West Flanders	25
Bruges, the Basilica of the Holy Blood	25
Bruges, the Jerusalem church	29
Gistel, Godelieve and het abbey	33
Province East Flanders	39
Melsele: Gaverland Chapel	39
Eksaarde, The chapel and her miraculous crosses	41
The old mountain of Geraardsberge	43
The seeress of Onkerzele	46
Denderwindeke, the chapel in the forest	49
Province Antwerp	51
From Antwerp to Schelle	51
Antwerp: our lady's Cathedral	51
Antwerp: the calvary of the Saint Paulus Church	56
Ranst, the solstice line of Millegem	59
Lier; in the footsteps of Saint Gummarus	61
The Saint Pieter's chapel	63

The church of Saint Gummarus	63
Emblem: two chapels, a well and a church	65
Geel; the church of Saint Dimpna	66
Zammel. the chapel of Saint Dimpna	68

Province of Flemish Brabant   69

Scherpenheuvel, from sacred tree of Basilica	69
Laken: two churches and a fountain	71
Halle and its Black Madonna	75
From Hakendover to Grimde	78

Province Limburg   81

Rutten: the sacred meadow and the chapel of Evermarus	81
The Holy House of Herstappe	82
Kuringen: the Abbey of Herkenrode	83
The holstones of Zonhoven	85

Wallonia   87

Province Walloon Brabant   87

The Abbey of Villers-la-Ville	87

Province Namur   89

The megaliths of Saint Mort	89

Province Luxembourg   93

The megaliths of Weris	93
The druids hill of Marche-en-Famenne	99
Spa: the footprint of Saint Remacle	100
The Abbey of Orval	103

Province Hainaut   107

Hollain, Pierre Brunehaut	107

Bibliography	111
Index	113

Introduction

Like almost everywhere over the last decades, also in Belgium there is a growing interest in a wide range of subjects generally classified under the term 'alternative sciences'. Quite a few people are looking for new values and a way of life that could help them develop spiritually.

They are searching for guidance, but sometimes they get lost in a mixture of ideas, experiences or esoteric communities of fellow seekers. However, it is during this quest for new values, that they also discover the ancient wisdom of our ancestors.

The ever-growing interest in the ancient nature religions and the rediscovery of traditions and seasonal celebrations attracted more and more people. Sun and moon are seen again as Divine Light Bearers and the earth as the Mother Goddess. Solstices and full moon phases are celebrated again, and the Celtic annual festivals are again important days on several calendars.

Trees, springs, rocks and minerals are viewed again in a different way. In the distant past stones were not considered as a dead material; sources were more than places where we could quench our thirst and trees more than suppliers of wood. They were honoured and also the particular place where they stood was very important. The practical application of customs and rituals created a sympathetic power with the natural elements of the visible and invisible world.

Much has changed since the Roman writer Pliny wrote these respectful words; 'Earth is the only part of nature which we gave the lovingly title of Mother. She receives us when we are born, she feeds us and at the end of our lives, when the rest of nature has rejected us forever, she takes us in her womb, and covers us like a mother. She is gentle, beneficent, indulgent and tender to the poor mortals that we are.'

To the rational thinking person, it remains hard to accept that the Earth is a living organism. Even more difficult to accept is that on that same earth, there are places where a special energy can be felt. Geological fault lines in the earth's surface forming a web of energy lines, where in the distant past ritual and ceremonial gatherings were held. Here lives the spirit of the earth.

Our ancestors knew and felt it all, but the ancient wisdom was completely neglected by our rational society. They were aware of those special places in the landscape. They felt that these places possessed a powerful energy, possibly for them, a divine energy. They also knew that it was not wise to live there, so they built the settlements always at a distance from that place of power.

However, behind the scenes of the well-known past, lays a range of feelings and thoughts of our ancestors of which we know a lot less. The line between awareness, enlightenment, consciousness and superstition, religion and magic was very thin and hard to describe. Worship and fear were close to each other, and spontaneously grown from both Christian and pagan concepts and preconceptions.

This book is meant as a signpost into unfamiliar territory and reintroduces us to that lost science. It's a guide for the individual seeker to rediscover the forgotten harmonious balance between men and the energy fields of the earth. There are, of course, far too many sites for them all to have been included in this book, so we have tried to select ones which can be visited now, and worth to see. There are GPS directions and references for the most difficult sites to locate.

So, let's make a journey to those many special places and energy lines in Belgium, the home of the author. Here also flows the energy of the earth through the landscape as invisible rivers through our daily lives. Despite the great influence of this energy on the human body, its existence has only become known in recent decades.

Ley lines

A network of straight tracks or 'leys' is considered to go through ancient sacred sites carrying a energy which was used to indicate routes and at their intersection stone circles, standing stones and mounds were erected.

Unfortunately, except for some in the south, there are only a few megaliths to be found in Belgium. With the arrival of Christianity most of them were destroyed and the first churches and chapels where built instead. This means that the oldest churches in Belgium, like in other places in Europe, also stand on ley lines.

Sometimes there are legends referring to the building site. A well-known legend is that of a Madonna statue that was found in a tree or a field. It happens that the person finding it, takes it home, but an invisible force lets it return to its finding place. This means that it will be honoured there and a chapel or church should be built on that place. On the other hand, there were several predetermined sites where a silk thread was stretched. Such legends are found by the dozen in Flanders, but give no historical certainty. However, many of these buildings mark still the energy points in the landscape.

It may even seem more important to absorb those places than to investigate; we still prefer an explanation for what really happens on those places and what we can feel. The specific places gives visitors not only energy, it also has a healing effect. However, when Googling, we see that there are several theories about ley lines.

After more than 30 years of research, I have built my own theory claiming there are three kinds of ley lines.

Firstly, the well-known 'leys' discovered by Alfred Watkins, the classical alignments of both pagan and Christian sites. Secondly, the astronomical leys, sites aligned in some important directions as the solstices or equinoxes.

At last, the most imported ley lines; the energy lines, natural phenomena which are nothing else than geological fault lines. The radiation from deep inside the earth reaches the surface by these fault lines so, in old churches we can find the same higher radiation level that we found on the most of the megalithic sites.

Ley lines can also be detected through air photography, which shows clearly the disrupted vegetation of different crops. Actually, most of the old roman roads in Belgium are laid on the old prehistoric paths and thus also on ley lines.

I have used a Geiger counter on hundreds of megalithic sites, old churches and chapels in Europe and I always found the same results, a radiation level much higher than the normal background radiation. We can ask now how our ancestors used those energies and how a high radiation level can be healthy.

I know that the word radiation scares most people and makes them think of Hiroshima, Chernobyl or more recently Fukushima, but radiation is also a natural phenomenon to be found everywhere on earth in different values. I will try to explain in a non-scientific way.

The normal background radiation in Belgium is 50 Becquerel (Bq is a unit to measure radiation). On most megalithic sites and in old churches built on ley lines, we can measure a value between 300 and 600 Bq. These Gamma-rays

Aerial photographs show clearly the ley lines in the landscape and the disturbed vegetation.

having an influence on the ionisation in the air. If people stay for a short time in such an environment their feel-good hormone serotonin will increase 40 percent within 10 minutes.

This energetic process that visitors often unconsciously experience makes those places suitable for self-development and meditation. I always tell people if you have a low energy level and you feeling down, go to that place or that particular church, and it will boost your mood. It's also an excellent natural method to reduce stress. Over the years a number of several visionary experiences, miraculous healings to intense feelings of joy or fear events have occurred in those places.

This thesis is fully confirmed by what the Canadian Michael Persinger, professor in neurosciences at the University of Ontario wrote down in; 'Space-time transients and unusual events'. Persinger noted that the influence of electromagnetic fields could lead to hallucinating or paranormal experiences. This immediately explains why our prehistoric ancestors chose those places for their rituals and healings, but also knew that it was not healthy to live there.
    Anyway, in the past, Stonehenge for example, was visited for his healing powers just like many other megaliths in Europe. It also explains why on many pilgrimage places like Lourdes in France, apparitions took place.

Dowsing

Dowsing is a craft of which the origins are as mysterious as the practice itself. Written records of divining can easily be traced back to 14th century Germany, but even earlier mentions have been found dating back to Herodotus the Greek in the 5th century B.C. One thing we do know, water divining has been around a long time and its precise origins remain a mystery.

Whenever and wherever divining was first discovered, man has always depended on the ability to locate clean, reliable sources of water for consumption and to irrigate crops. Exactly when someone first attempted to divine water remains unclear, but other sources claim that throughout history water divining has captured the interest and imagination of great minds such as Leonardo da Vinci, Isaac Newton and Albert Einstein.

Dowsing or divining has been practised for centuries throughout the world not only as a method for finding water; it has been proved that the technique can be applied to find ley lines. The current theory to explain it is that energy which comes from water or the electro-magnetic field of the earth which rises vertically above them can be picked up by the dowser either by holding a Y-shaped dowsing rod or two L-shaped rods or by a pendulum.
   Divining rods do not contain the power of divination. The ability is found in the diviner. It is assumed that everyone has the potential to dowse and it is not a unique gift given to a select few.

Most used are L-shaped divining rods (also called 'angle rods') crafted of copper. Brass rods are also commonly used. Rods of different thicknesses and lengths are chosen as a matter of preference once the individual determines which works best for them. The short end is held in the hand and the long end is pointed outward.
   The typical response from L-shaped rods involves the rotation of the rods in the hands of the user. They can rotate inward and cross to form an 'X' which typically indicates a positive or 'yes' response. Lack of movement typically indicates a negative or 'no' response. If desired, the rods can also

rotate together and give an indication of direction, examples include locating magnetic north or determining the direction of flow for an underground water source.

In addition to metal rods, Y-shaped tree branches from willow, hazel or birch trees are also used. In this case, the user holds the top of the 'Y' in his hands and points the base of the Y forward. A positive response to a ley line or water would involve the base of the Y bending toward the ground to indicate location.

Dowsers have discovered that ley lines and ancient sacred sites radiated powerful forces which affect our well-being. Our prehistoric ancestors were natural dowsers who did not require anything to detect this energy but could feel it in their bodies because of their keen sensitivity to nature. The meridian pattern of ley lines and their intersection, particularly at specific sacred sites, is purported to be analogous to the acupuncture system of the human body.

Let us start our journey through unknown Belgium now. Whether it is for spiritual refreshment or physical recreation, it can be a purposeful and beautiful excursion that restores us in soul en body. The special locations discussed in this book are also the result of almost thirty years of research backed with scientific material, but also using dowsing rods. The search continues and regularly new and exciting places discovered.

Dowsing with L-shaped rods; left the search position, right the found position.

The power of the places

In the 7th century, our areas were Christianized and pagan practices integrated into Christianity. The reason why the early church fathers used various pagan places of worship was twofold. The first one was to erase the ancient science of the energetic forces of the Earth from the memory of the common people; the other was to transform the same energy into the new sanctuaries.

The energy lines were obscured by spicy stories of many saints and the healing , from now on, would come only from prayer and no longer from the spirits of nature or the strength of the place. The orientation of churches and chapels were therefore carefully determined and followed the direction of the energy lines.

The simplicity of the illiterate that lived here was played upon in a subtle and thoughtful way.

The impressive and miraculous stories that were told about the apostles who converted the pagans became the basis for the position of various churches. Sources where a cult existed, were taken over by the new belief, the source became in many cases a baptism font. The worship of sacred trees was tolerated by putting a Madonna statue in them. The pagan festivities were getting also a Christian character.

Megaliths were destroyed or incorporated into Christianity, but due to lack of chauvinism in our country, the remaining stones disappear for agricultural and urban development.

Countless churches and chapels were built on the old pagan places that were being perceived as sacred. After over 300 year's repentance offensive, the church had begun to react with violence against all shortcomings and remnants of paganism. Superstition had to be fought. If this could not be done by preaching, then it would be obtained by prosecution and punishment.

Saints at the right place

For our distant ancestor's nature was loaded with supernatural powers and animated with an animus. The popular belief that had arisen from animistic thinking was not a naive belief or illusion, but a force that was based on connectedness. Animism is therefore sometimes regarded as the oldest religion on earth.

Part of this belief was the sympathy or signature doctrine, not only the science of the ancient pagans, but it was also used in the following popular devotion. The book of nature, one of the Books of Revelation make this clear. God created plants in the shape of human organs to heal those organs with similar shapes. Both in the writings of Hildegard von Bingen as in those of Paracelsus is repeatedly shown that the relationship between medicine and theology was quite normal.

The lungwort heals the lungs, Judas's ear the ears and the walnut is beneficial for brains because they have the same shape. Baer's breech has deep grooves that appear on nerves and was used to cure diseases. Red flowers healed blood diseases, yellow flowers jaundice.

But times are changing. Many churches are famous for the miraculous healings where certain saints are worshiped and called upon for the most different ailments or diseases. It seems that God had endowed some saints with certain special powers. The altar and statues where the people prayed were given a privileged place in the church.

The people went on pilgrimage to cure their diseases and discomforts and sought help by the so-called healing saints. It was guided by the name and the external characteristics of that particular saint who was called upon for help. Al those saints were martyrs whose bizarre life could be the theme for a novel or a horrible tragic drama. They all died in a sadistic way, during their lives even some form of masochism was never far away.

Saint Blasius was called upon to cure skin diseases and is shown with a hook ripping open his body. Saint Denis was called for all sorts of illnesses of the head because he was beheaded, and is shown with his head in his hands. Saint Lawrence, who was martyred on a grid over a burning fire, was called upon by those who are plagued by burning skin ailments. The Holy Appolonia cures toothache because the teeth were pulled out and her jaw shattered during her torture.

For heart disease, they went to Saint Augustine because he is depicted with his heart in his hands. Holy Godelieve of Gistel is invoked against throat ailments because she was strangled, but also against blindness because a blind born girl regained sight by her intervention.

Saint Christopher is called to calm down crying and screaming children because it is believed that he helped the Child Jesus to cross the river. Because of this he becomes the protector and patron saint of travellers.

Saint Denis with his head in his hands and the Holy Appolonia with a pincer holding one of her teeth.

Saint Donat, the protector against lightning.

The Holy Rita is called upon in hopeless cases, usually marriage problems. The reason is clear. Before her entry into the convent she had lead an unhappily married life!

Certain saints are even called upon to obtain favourable weather. In West Flanders farmers called the Holy Drogo for the weather to become dry weather. To get sunshine, eggs were brought to the monastery of the Poor Clare in honour of Saint Clare. Usually this happened to obtain a sunny day on a marriage. Saint Donat, the Christian version of the Germanic Thor, was consulted to protect the house from lightning.

The fourteen most important Healing Saints. We find their statues always placed on ley lines.

Miraculous healings

If a saint had been buried on a particular place and his skeleton or parts of his bones were kept in the church, everything was done to touch them. People who hoped for healing would lie down on his grave or some earth from under the tombstone was pulled by hand, which was rubbed on the diseased body parts. Often, a bit of sand was taken home where it was drunk mixed with water, or as a talisman worn around the neck in a little bag.

There was also a healing power granted to the dust on the tombstone and the water droplets that condensed on the cold stone slabs of the tomb of these healing saints. Some tombstones were even scraped and the released powder was eaten.

Many pilgrims would pray on their knees or stretch in a cross shape on the ground. The quest for direct contact with the earth is also unmistakably from the fact that some pilgrims would crawl on their knees to the place of worship. For that reason absorbing the sacred power from earth was very important. Then, the faithful put its sacrifice as close as possible to the statue or the tomb of the saint.

An angel with the relics of a healing saint.

Bad athmosphere

The intense worship usually took place was to obtain a favour or healing, often resulting in a lot of trouble and sorrow accumulating, especially when candles are burned in a chapel dedicated to Our Lady.

For century's sick people leaving behind their pain and sorrow visited these chapels. This kind of heavy atmosphere can be felt at various places and under different forms.

For believers, it was always taboo to light a candle with another candle. They always use matches because the possibility exists that they would take over the disease or misery of the other person. Some mistrust is encountered,

because they always keep their own candle as far away as possible from the already lit candle.

So here we find undoubtedly a variant of the old use to bind a piece of cloth to a tree, which shouldn't be removed by anyone.

Dragons and green men

Every ecclesiastical building had some images in common, but there were variations depending on local history and traditions. Mostly, the basic common imagery of good and evil is expressed in a mixture of Celtic, Germanic and Romanesque sculptural forms. However, it is certain that the masons of that time may have incorporated some of their own ideas.

In countless cathedrals and churches we find images of a dragon accompanied by dragon slayers like Saint Michael and Saint George. It is known that it was the core business of those two, but also countless other local saints are famous for slaying a dragon. Just like in other places in Europe, the dragon symbolizes not the evil but the force the earth.

In almost every culture, the dragon was associated with the power lines in the earth crust. The dragon, since ancient times called in China 'chi' and Japan 'ki', was the vital life force of the earth and equal to the 'Wouivre', the earth snake or dragon energy of the western druids.

Another common image that we find is the 'Green Man'. It is the image of a face that has vegetation growing out of its openings; mouth, nose, ears and sometimes the eyes. It is usually surrounded by a wreath of oak leaves.

We find it carved in stone or wood or painted on windows. Sometimes at the entrance, on the ceiling, on pillars or passageways, or somewhere hidden in a corner. The Green Man also has many faces. Sometimes demonic, sometimes sad or with a peaceful expression. Due to the high prevalence in churches it is speculated that the early medieval sculptors though they usually had been converted to Christianity, still had a pagan character. Both, the Green Man and the Dragon symbolise the fertility and intelligence within nature.

Everywhere present in churches built on ley lines, the green man and dragon slayers Saint George or Saint Michaël.

Provinces of Belgium

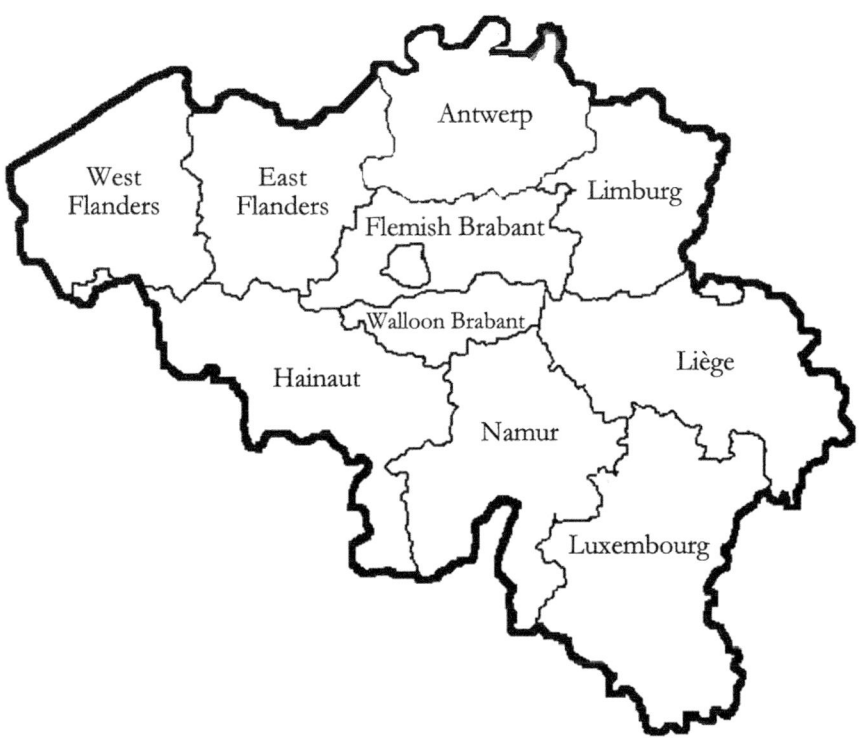

Flanders

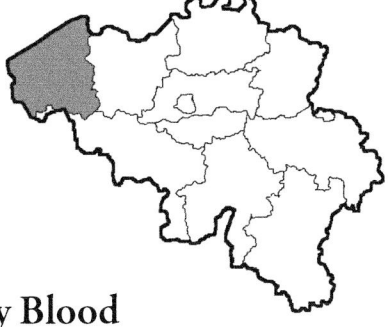

Province West Flanders

Bruges, the Basilica of the Holy Blood

Brugge 8000, Burg
51°12'29.30"N – 3°13'36.29"E

Bruges, also called 'the Venice of the North' is famed for its beauty. It's a popular tourist destination among British travellers, due to its close proximity to the major port of Zeebrugge, and because it is the first city in Belgium. The city has much to offer, many interesting churches, a nice Market Square, a Belfry and there are several powerful ley lines. We will discuss here two of the most important places.

On the Burg Square stands one of the most important buildings in the city. The Basilica of the Holy Blood (De Heilig Bloedbasiliek) contains one of the holiest relics in Christianity; a small cylinder with blood, reputed to be that of Christ, brought to Bruges in the early 12th century from Jerusalem, during the Crusades.

According to the legend, the Templars would have found the Precious Blood of Christ on Christmas Day 1148, in the Holy Sepulchre in the presence of Derrick of Alsace (Diederik van de Elzas) and his wife Sybilla of Anjou. Sybilla had been infected with leprosy and was suffering from a heavy fever.

The entrance of the Basilica on the Burg Square.

But when she held the relic in her hands, she had a vision in which she saw Bruges as 'the New Jerusalem of the West' and she cured miraculously. She made a solemn pledge to turn Bruges into a Holy City and when the couple came home, the masons just had finished the Chapel of Saint Basil.

The basilica was built between 1134 and 1157 and consists of a Romanesque lower chapel and a Gothic upper chapel. The two levels are very different from each other; the Romanesque lower level dates from the first half of the 12th century and is dedicated to Saint Basilius. It is austere with very little decoration.

Before we enter this chapel, we pass a statue of Christ on the Cold Stone. The bronze statue has very shiny knees because of the rubbing of the knees before entering the chapel should bring good luck. Next, we pass 'the Tomb of Christ', with on the

Christ on the cold stone with his shiny knees and the Tomb of Christ in the lower chapel.

The chalice on the tombstone in the lower chapel.

right side strange carvings in the wall. Is it the Holy Grail?

The doorway connects the right aisle with the nave and has a small-sculpted tympanum depicting the baptism of Saint Basil. The right aisle also contains a polychrome statue of the Madonna and Child, displayed behind glass.

The chapel has an oblong nave supported by four heavy pillars.

The feeble light, which enters through the few windows, creates a strange atmosphere. At the left of the choir is a Pieta with in front of it, two black tombstones in the floor with the image of a chalice, or is it again a reference to the grail? However, here is the most energetic place of the whole chapel.

The Gothic upper chapel is full of colour and details. There are nicely stained glass windows and a brightly painted altar backdrop depicting the Trinity and scenes relating to the Holy Blood relic. The back wall of the side chapel displays ex-voto's of those whose prayers before the Holy Blood have been answered. A monumental staircase from 1533 connects the two chapels, the time during which also the facade was built.

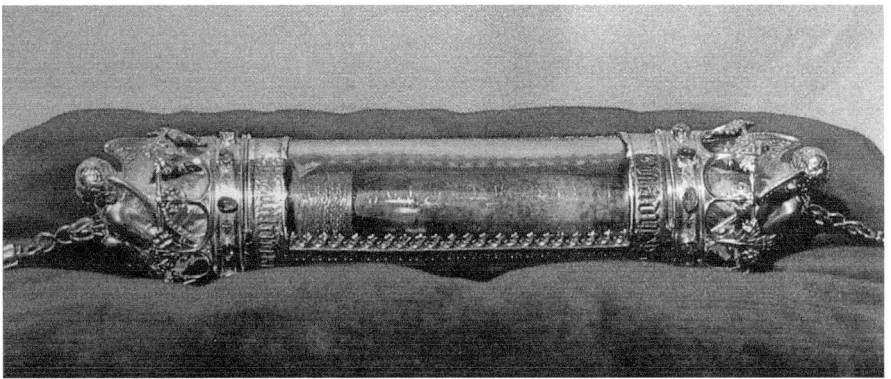

The relic of the Precious Blood.

The Holy Blood Relic contains a piece of cloth with the Blood of Christ. It is embedded in a rock-crystal vial, which is placed inside a small glass cylinder capped with a golden crown. The relic is kept in a magnificent silver tabernacle with a sculpture of the Lamb of God in the large side chapel of the upper church. Since arriving in Bruges, the vial has never been opened. The Precious Blood is still being displayed every Friday, before and after the mass, to be venerated by the faithful for the most various reasons.

The colourful Procession of the Holy Blood is still paraded around the town in an ancient ceremony every Ascension Day. Some fifty thousand pilgrims are present to see the bishop of Bruges carrying the relic through the streets, accompanied by more than 1800 costumed residents re-enacting historical and biblical scenes.

This old tradition dates from 1291. It followed a route around the city walls until 1578, when due to the religious wars its relocation was necessitated to the city centre. It is this route that is still followed today.

The famous Flemish priest-poet Guido Gezelle who was born in Bruges described the city as a copy of the Holy Land, with its great Gothic churches called Jerusalem, Nazareth or Bethlehem and of course, because of the Holy Blood that was brought here during the crusades.

Bruges, the Jerusalem Church

Brugge 8000, Peperstraat
51°12'44.64"N – 3°14'1.28"E

The Jerusalem Church is the place to be for mystery hunters. What could have possessed someone to build such a church here? It is maybe the most remarkable of all the churches in Bruges. Anselmus Adornes and his wife, merchants from Genoa, built it in the 15th century as a scale model of the church of the Holy Sepulchre in Jerusalem.

This intriguing building is renowned for its massive form and the large globe on its tower. Furthermore, we find a Jerusalem Cross (previously Maltese cross) and a broken Saint Catherine Wheel. Left and right are oriental turrets depicting the sun and the moon.

Inside it is also a really strange church. We find an original late medieval example of the Calvary, with the tools by which Christ was tortured, the cock (that crowed three times), three skulls and bones. Further, a sacrament tower and a reliquary cross. Lovely stained glass windows and memorial paintings on the walls symbolize the different members of the Adornes family.

On the stained glass windows and on the walls of the church are painted clouds pierced by rays of light. According to the prophet Isaiah at the end of time, when clouds darken the earth, the light will shine on the New Jerusalem.

On either side of the Calvary is a fourteen-step staircase leading to the Saint Catherine Chapel.

Also in Jerusalem there was a stand above the crypt, which was accessible through a double staircase with fourteen steps. Fourteen is the symbolic number of ancestors of Christ and the Cross; the church used later the symbolic number 14 for the number of stations.

The Jeruzalem Church with his strange towers capped with sun and moon symbols.

However, the eye catcher is the freestanding tomb of Anselmus Adornes and his wife Margaret. The design of this tomb connects with some other 15th century detached tombs in Bruges, of which only that of Mary of Burgundy in the Our Lady's Church has been preserved until this day.

Already in 1470, before he left Bruges, Adornes had written his will and arranged his funeral.

He had written in his will that of his tomb bearing his image, the head had to be turned towards the light and that at the same time the axis of the building had to lie on the north-south meridian.

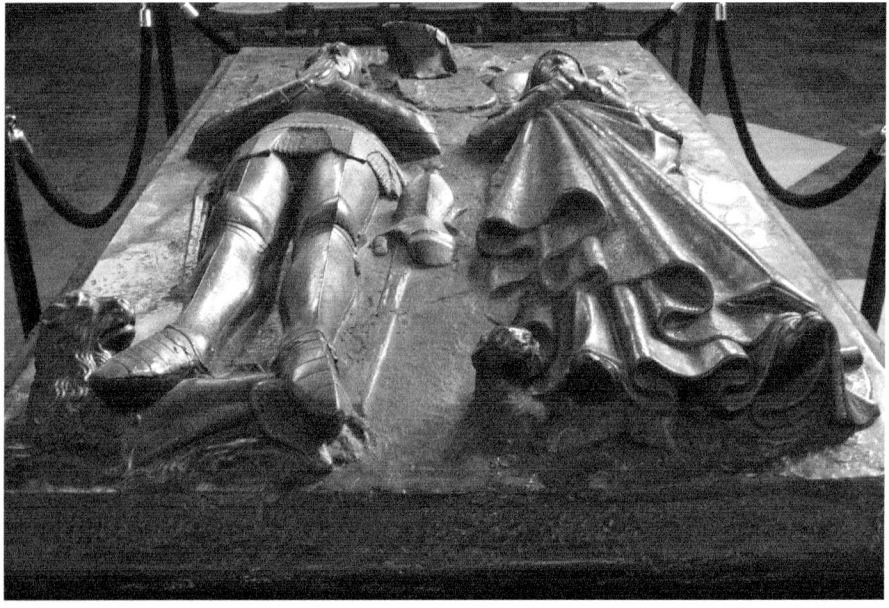

The weird interior of the church with the tomb of Anselmus Adornes and his wife.

Moreover, every afternoon, but at the time of Saint John Festival in the summer, a sunspot lit his face. During the midwinter in December the light falls again on the tomb at sunrise, but through the open gate. The chapel, like symbolism also suggests, is not directed to the East (Jerusalem) as they had expected, but at the contrary to the poles. This tomb and the imitation of the crypt of the Holy Sepulchre provide this remarkable funerary chapel with a distinct character.

At the left and right of the entrance to the second part, a praying chapel where services are still being held is situated. On the right side is the access to the crypt where you can find the body of Christ behind an iron framework. To enter one must be able to bend forwards, possibly this was done to show respect.

According to history, the brothers Peter and Jake Adornes wanted to make a true copy of the Holy Sepulchre in Bruges. Everything was well planned so the construction was perfect, until the moment they wanted to copy the crypt. The stone that had to cover the tomb had the same size as those in Jerusalem, but when they put it in its place, it broke in two pieces.

A second stone suffered the same fate. It was as if the devil had been involved in it, also this stone broke at the same place as the first. Only one solution had been considered, travel back to Jerusalem and re-measure the stone. There they found that the stone on the Holy Sepulchre was broken at the same place as the stone in Bruges.

It is not certain if the church is a true and faithful imitation of the building in Jerusalem, because the Holy Sepulchre in Jerusalem was destroyed by fire during the 16th century. On the other hand, it is historically accurate that Jake and Peter Adornes have undertaken two trips to Jerusalem.

However, it is also certain that Anselmus travelled – in connection with the wool trade – several times to Scotland, where King James III raised him as knight in the order of the Unicorn. In the aftermath of the death of Charles the Bold fate fared him not so well. After he had been imprisoned there for a short time, he decided to leave Bruges.

Back in Scotland, there was another civil war going on and he had got the command of the troops who were guarding the Royal Castle. On January 25, 1483 during a pilgrimage Anselmus was killed by rebels. His body was buried in Saint Michael's Church at Linlithgow Palace in Scotland but his heart was transferred to Bruges and buried in the tomb in the Jerusalem church.

Without doubt a very strange story and an even stranger church. All the symbolism within and outside the church had clearly intended to go further than just building a remake of the Holy Sepulchre in Jerusalem. No, Adornes wanted a New Jerusalem in Bruges and the church would be the centre of it.

This unique church gives you a chance to experience a truly old place of worship and explore its many nooks and crannies. Many ley lines connect al the old churches in Bruges this means that also the building place for the Jeruzalem Church was purposely chosen.

Gistel, Godelieve and her Abbey

Gistel 8470, Abdijstraat
51° 8'57.96"N – 2°55'36.05"E

The Holy Godelieve from Gistel is until today the most revered saint in West Flanders. That her worship is still very much alive is confirmed by the many pilgrims who annually come to visit the Abbey Ten Putte. Her sad story was described by a monk from French Flanders in the north of France. We read that Godelieve was born around 1052 in Boulogne and belonged to a noble family. At the young age of seventeen, she had to marry Bertolf, the son of the lord of Gistel, probably for political reasons.

The differences between the couple were very big. Bertolf was a rough man from Friesland who had settled in the region. From pagan he converted to Christianity but did not take standards and rules too seriously. Godelieve however, was a civilized and noble girl with refined manners who lived her faith with conviction.

Bertolf had little interest in his devout wife, was looking for fun and entertainment with different other women. After some time he decided for Godelieve to live with his mother, but she drove her from the castle and to the farm, where she had to live between the servants and the maids and was continuously humiliated.

Godelieve fled back to her parental home. Her father complained to the bishop of Tournai and the Count of Flanders and under pressure from church and state and to avoid excommunication.
    Bertolf promised to treat her well, as good men have to do. But then, Bertolf forged a diabolical plan with his mother to get rid of Godelieve. While he made a short trip to Bruges he gave his servants the order to murder her. She was strangled with a scarf the next night.

To ensure that she was dead her head was held in the water of the nearby water well. While the assassins carried her body home, the dark paving stones they walked on coloured snow white. Godelieves lifeless body was returned to her chamber. When she was found the next day, the lash of the strangling was clearly visible, but the law did nothing. Bertolf, finally freed from his pious woman, let her bury in the chapel.

After the death of Godelieve it did not take long for Bertolf to remarry. Before his second wife died after thirteen years of marriage she had given him a daughter Edith, who was blind since birth. The legend tells that at one day Edith went to the chapel to pray on the tombstone of her mother to heal from blindness. A miracle happened; Edith was able to see and determine immediately that she had not prayed on the tombstone of her mother but on that of Godelieve. In gratitude for this miracle, Edith is said to have founded an abbey on the place where Godelieve was killed and became the first abbess of it.

The strangulation of Godelieve on a stained glass window in the church of Gistel.

There is also a peculiar legend that led to Bertolf's repentance. Bertolf had sent one of his servants to Gistel with linen to make shirts. On the road to the abbey where we now find a little chapel, the boy saw a woman along the roadside while sewing. When she asked him where he was going, he told her that he had to go to a tailor in Gistel. 'You don't have to walk that far' said the woman, 'give the linen to me. I know Lord Bertolf well enough and he'll be happy because I have sewn a lot for him and he always liked my outstanding work'. The servant went back to the castle to tell the good news to his boss but unlike what he expected; Bertolf was very angry that he had given the precious textile to a stranger!

'What's her name?' I did not ask muttered the frightened servant. 'What does she look like?' Very astonished he heard the description of Godelieve. 'That must be an impostor,' Bertolf roared. 'Get out and go retrieve that linen!'

But it was not a fraud because the young woman sat sewing diligently at her place beside the road. The shirt was just about ready, neatly folded and handed to the servant. 'Can I have your name,' asked the servant, 'because the master has asked for it'.

'That is not necessary' was the reply, 'if he looks at the shirt, he will immediately know who made it. Tell him that he no longer can resist God's mercy and to do penance.' She said goodbye to the boy and disappeared.

Bertolf recognizes the work of Godelieve and rushes to the place where the servant met her but of course, she was gone. And this became her greatest miracle, the conversion of her unworthy husband and murderer. Under the influence of the miracles at her tombstone and those happened by the well pit, Bertolf turned to repentance. He undertook a pilgrimage to Rome and stayed as a devout man in the abbey of Saint Winoksbergen in France, where he died.

The people began to worship Godelieve very soon afterwards as a saint. Numerous miracles were attributed to her and only 14 years after her death she was declared sacred by the bishop of Tournai. Today she is invoked against throat and eye diseases and especially as protector and keeper of domestic peace and marital fidelity.

The pelgrimage

The annual pilgrimage is an ancient custom. It takes place between the period of Godelieve's name day on July 6 and July 25, the day she was strangled. July 6 is very important for the pilgrims because then the shrine and the well are blessed. Everyone drinks the curative water and washes the eyes with it. From there it takes us to the chapel, where the story of the woven shirt without a seam happens. The so called Sew Chapel is along the road that connects the Abbey with the church of Gistel.

Very special indeed is the 'seamless shirt,' which according to legend was made by Godelieve and still visible in

The well with the curative water.

The small hill with the powerful Crow Chapel.

the abbey. The famous shirt was woven of 'byssus' flax from the valley of the Nile.

Along with the suspected 'tunic' of Jesus in the cathedral of Trier, it is the only known piece that was made this way.

Another stop on the pilgrimage is the Crow's Chapel, located on a small hill and named after a legend in the life of Godelieve. Bertolf had instructed her to drive away the crows that fed on the grain from the fields. Obediently she performed her task, but one day she heard the church bells ringing and like other believers she wanted to attend mass. She chased the crows in the barn and asked them to stay there until she had returned. The good birds did nicely what she had asked.

The abbey Ten Putte is still visited by both pilgrims and tourists. In the beautiful domed chapel is the well-pit from 1634 with the miraculous water. You can visit the abbey church, the devotion chapel and pilgrims walk three times around the Crow Chapel and three times around the statue of Godelieve on the place where she was murdered. Especially recommended is a visit to the museum where you learn more about the saint and the history of the abbey.

The beautiful abbey domain with its white buildings and lush garden is an oasis of tranquillity but also ley lines cross the abbey property in different directions. The most energetic place is the small hill where we find the Crow Chapel. Another ley runs through the Abbey Street along the Sew Chapel to the church in the village. Here we find besides seven miracle paintings also the relic-holders with the bones and the skull of Godelieve. The church with dragons left and right to the entrance is also a special power spot.

Left, Goddelieve with the shirt on an old pilgrimage image and right, the 'seamless shirt' that still can be admired in the abbey.

Province East Flanders

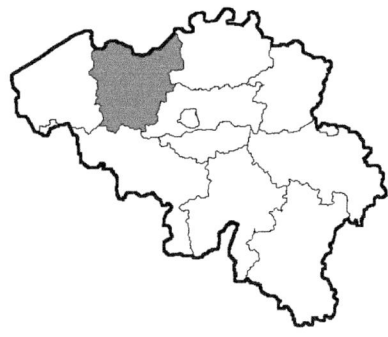

Melsele: Gaverland Chapel

Melsele 9120, Gaverlandstraat
51°13'33.28"N – 4°16'2.59"E

The neo-Gothic chapel is oriented towards the direction of the summer solstice and located on the straight track 'Kapelwegel'. The history of this place of worship originated in the 16th century when a family from Melsele discovered a black wooden statue in a lime tree. It was a 1 meter high Madonna with Jesus on the left arm. They decided to place it against the church wall, so the priest would find it and give it a place in the church. Great was their amazement as they found it the next morning on the same place in the lime. The statue was taken back three times from the tree, but each time the next morning it returned to the same place. The neighbourhood was very soon informed and believes that the Blessed Virgin would be honoured on this place.

A first small chapel, barely fifteen square meters, was built at the site where the miraculous statue was worshipped. In 1665 the chapel was enlarged, but during French rule completely destroyed. Fortunately, the statue was saved and a new chapel was constructed in 1840. In May 1864, a new chapel was consecrated, but again it did not meet expectations because it was still too small for the

The neo-gothic pilgrimage chapel with a sick tree at the backside.

growing number of pilgrims. When the mill next door burned down, there was space to increase the chapel once again. It would be double in size from the previous one this time.

Several miraculous healings were attributed to Our Lady of Gaverland. A shattered leg of a seven year old boy had to be amputated, but his parents went on pilgrimage to Gaverland as last hope. The leg healed so rapidly that the boy could walk back home on his own.

Another miracle was that of Johanna, a four year old blind girl. After having consulted all the doctors, her parents went on a pilgrimage to Gaverland. During the second day of the novena, the girl could see again. Similar cures and other favours were obtained to derive the many ex-voto's in the chapel. The chapel of Gaverland had formerly been a lonely place, but it is now situated between traffic and buildings. However, the remarkably strong energetic field inside the chapel clearly shows traces of deformities in the trees on the square in front of it.

Eksaarde, the chapel and her miraculous crosses

Eksaarde (Lokeren) 9160, Kruiskapeldreef
51° 9'35.00"N – 3°58'42.75"E

The desolate Cross Chapel (Kruiskapel) of Eksaarde has a remarkable history. In the 14th century, the story of Madonna statues found in trees seems to have been updated. No trees on this place because this chapel was built on the place where two miraculous crosses were found.

A curious legend states that a farmer that bumped into two crosses while digging in his field. Surprisingly he saw that blood flowed from one of the crosses he had hit. He decided to take them home, but when he came past the church, the bells suddenly began to ring.

The strange story soon spread. The Mayor claimed them as his property and took them to his castle in Hontenisse, but without explanation they were returned to the field. The people from the village saw it as the divine desire that the two crosses would be honoured in their grounds.

A copy of one of the crosses is now on display in the church of Eksaarde, the other one in the Cross Chapel. They show the image of the crucified Jesus

The desolate Cross Chapel and Well.

One of the miraculous Crosses.

and probably date from the 11th or 12th century. The 'wound', as it was made by the spade, is still visible. The most remarkable fact of this legend is that the crosses consist of a metal alloy of which the composition is said to be completely unknown. Also, it has been tried several times to paint the crosses gold or silver, but every attempt failed.

The Cross Chapel is orientated north-east. It was built in 1626 at the place where the crosses were found in 1317. In front of the chapel we find the 'Holy Well'. This also bears a secret, because nobody would ever be able to determine the depth. This highly energetic place clearly possesses the features of a pre-Christian source cult.

The old mountain of Geraardsbergen

Geraardsbergen 9500, Oudeberg
50°46'20.89"N – 3°53'25.03"E

Located on the outskirts of the town of Geraardsbergen in the Flemish Ardennes, this 110 meters high hill is one of the highest points of Flanders. The name 'Oudenberg' or 'Old Mountain' speaks for itself. Some historians refer the origin of this name to Odinberg, the Supreme God of the old Germanics. This is very well possible, because the Old Mountain still is a place where different pagan traditions are being practised.

The annual ritual 'Tonnekensbrand' (burning the barrel) is well known, during which an ancient custom is still being honoured. On the first Sunday of spring, a barrel with tar burns is put on the hilltop to celebrate the death of winter and to welcome the awakening of nature. The Celtic fire festival is therefore still present.

Also a source is located on the mountain, and according to local historians, a pagan sacrificial site containing a dolmen was to be found. The ancient peoples had a great veneration for sources and especially for those at the Old Mountain, of which the origin was inexplicable. There had to be celebrated and sacrificed to the water Goddess.

According to legend, a sacrifice was held by throwing bread and fish into the pond, and the pagan priest or druid would subsequently drink the cup with wine in which a fish swam. First, the pagan sacrificial table (such as the dolmen was formerly called) was smeared with the blood of the sacrificed animal and then sprinkled it onto the people there to let them share in the ritual.
    We still know this ritual today as the sprinkling of holy water, as it has been incorporated by Christianity and by burning candles during the church service.

The chapel, dedicated to Our Lady on the Old Mountain was built in 1906. In the 7th century, when the region was Christianized, it is assumed that a first wooden chapel has been built.
    This is a not so spectacular event, so there is a more impressive version that tells how the chapel landed on the mountain. The legend tells that a certain Jan Tanton on his way to Bruges was overtaken by a heavy storm during which his fellow travellers were hit dead by lightning.

The chapel as it looks today.

Jan sank in prayer and promised to build a chapel on the mountain if he was allowed to return to Bruges alive, what actually happened. He kept his promise and settled on the mountain where he lived as a hermit.

The chapel was built in its present form since the former not only was dilapidated but had become too small. During the inauguration of the new chapel there were more than twelve thousand pilgrims present. It became a true place of pilgrimage because of the miracle that took place in 1760. According to legend, a coach with pilgrims who were returning from Halle to worship to Our Lady encountered serious problems.

Some of the brakes on the rear wheels broke and the horses trotted of the Old Mountain with a hellish speed. The panicked occupants called upon Our Lady for help and their prayers were answered instantly, because an angel suddenly appeared from heaven. He took the reins of the horses and brought them immediately to a standstill. A painting of this miraculous salvation can still be seen in the chapel.

The worship of the statue of Mary reached its peak during the cholera epidemic that ravaged the region in 1849. Thousands of pilgrims turned to her with many healings as result. Since then the statue is visited as a cure for all kinds of diseases, consolation and support. Deduced from the hundreds of ex-voto's that fill the walls of the chapel, hundreds of people have found healing here.

Though the hill becomes a completely Christian place of pilgrimage, the ancient pagan rites are still celebrated annually on the last Sunday of February. It starts with the parade with over 800 participants that portray historic scenes from the birth of the city. After the litany of Our Lady by the Dean, the mayor, aldermen and councillors drink wine containing a live fish from a sixteenth-century silver cup. Here we find back a blend of the old pagan libation: the wine (blood) is considered the abode of the soul, but also the wisdom, the fish symbolizes the new life.

On the hill behind the chapel starts the throwing of the pretzels. Ten thousand ring-shaped biscuits fly into the crowd where everyone secretly hopes to catch that one golden pretzel worth 750 euro. At 8 pm at the festival ends with the 'Tonnekensbrand' that is answered by other bonfires on the hills of the surrounding villages.

That the chapel of the Old Mountain is a very energetic place is proven by the numerous acknowledgments that we find inside, and the several miraculous healings that took place. However, it is strange that the chapel, built in the beginning of last century is not oriented to the east, but northeast. Was this consciously done to take into account the geological conditions? It forms the hub of six ley lines of which the most imported runs to the church of Onkerzele in the north-east.

The seeress of Onkerzele

Onkerzele 9500, Onkerzelestraat
50°46'57.19"N – 3°54'40.29"E

At the end of 1932, the south of Belgium must have been quite popular by Our Lady because she appeared in Beauraing no fewer than thirty times to five children between 9 and 15 years old. The apparitions occurred at dusk in a hawthorn near the so called Grotto of Lourdes. The first apparition took place on 19 November and the last on 3 January 1933.

After Beauraing, our lady appeared in Banneux at eight occasions between January 15th and March 2nd 1933 to Mariette Beco, an 11 year old girl. As with most appearances, the children were not believed. However, the sites became later well-known places of pilgrimage.

After she had appeared in Ham-sur-Sambre, Rochefort, Chaineux, Tubize and Verviers, the Virgin visited several places in Flanders. There were appearances in Wilrijk, Lokeren, Etikhoven, Olsene, Berchem and Wielsbeke. In the village of Onkerzele, Mary appeared repeatedly to Leonie Van den Dyck, a simple housewife and mother of 13 children.

Leonie, known as 'Nieken' in the neighbourhood, became the most famous inhabitant of Onkerzele. After the first appearance she had visions and began to make predictions. She predicted the death of King Albert I whom she had seen being pushed of a cliff. The death of Albert did not occur by accident, but murder has never been proven, but is still considered by many as the truth. Further, she predicted the death of Queen Astrid in 1935, the outbreak of World War II and foretold that after her death her body would not dissolve, but would be kept intact.

Leonie died on 23 June 1949. In 1972, more than twenty years after her death, her body was excavated in the presence of the camera crew from the famous and popular TV program Echo. What Leonie had predicted was true and hit everyone with surprise, her body was still intact. This made her apparitions and visions not only accepted by her followers, but also by many others. During her life even more striking events took place. At times, she wore stigmata wounds and during the funeral of a child, she would weep, leaving her tears crystallized.

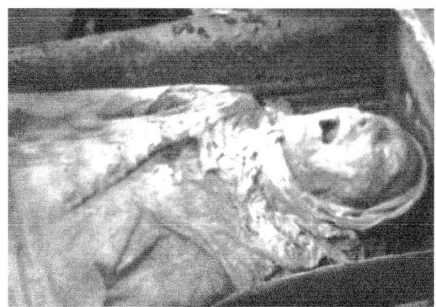

Leonie during her excavation in 1972

The most remarkable were her predictions about the course of World War II and the barbaric massacres at the end of the war. 'Many people will lose their lives because whole cities will be destroyed. Many people are being slaughtered in a way worse than ever been done to animals. Daily endless caravans of people are driven to death as if it were useless objects. Others let people starve and die a horrible death. The horrors will soon reach their peak and once peace returns, the world will be overwhelmed and speechless.' It is clear that Leonie meant the horror of concentration camps and the extermination of the Jews.

Her life, apparitions, visions and revelations were recorded in a thick book, 'The Wondrous Life of Leonie van den Dyck'. But even so, there was little or no attention from the ecclesiastical authorities for the appearances in Onkerzele, there were plenty of reasons for the population of the town to keep the devotion to Mary alive.

The last miraculous healing dates from not so long ago. A girl's grandmother regularly went to the tomb of the visionary to pray for the healing of her grandchild. The girl had been suffering from advanced bone cancer and was unexpectedly cured in 2006.

Leonie van den Dyck next to the rock chapel where she had her appearances. Right, the chapel with in the background the church of Onkerzele.

Therefore the bishop received a medical report of the healings being investigated by a board of doctors commissioned by the church. Currently, a long and possibly difficult and disappointing procedure has been initiated in order to obtain the beatification of Leonie.

It is quite evident that disappointment awaits. Medjugorje in southern Bosnia-Herzegovina is currently the most visited Catholic shrine but is still not recognized by the official church. This is a paradoxical attitude, because the same church gave it the status of holy place. Although millions of patients and doctors have visited Lourdes and at least 3500 healings have been stated as supernatural, only 65 have been accepted by the church as a miracle.

Finally, we may suggest that there might be two causes at the origin of the apparitions that took place in both Onkerzele and elsewhere. Usually, Mary appeared to children or to highly sensitive, but also simple, uncomplicated personalities. They repeatedly went back to the place of their first appearance and spent many hours in rapture, worship and prayer. Only there, they got their visions. Was this attraction determined by the influence of the place, or by what they felt unconsciously? Let's have a look at where all this took place.

In Onkerzele, the apparitions mostly occurred at the rock chapel built in 1877, on the edge of the hill on which the village church stands. Here runs the same powerful ley line, also found on the 'Oudenberg' in Geraardsbergen.
    The sensitivity of the characters and the deep Christian conviction during this period, combined with the energetic aspect of the place, has explained the cause of the appearances in both Onkerzele as in many other places.

In the churchyard the grave of Leonie remains at the present time a true place of pilgrimage. The fact that her body was preserved also stands in connection with the electromagnetic radiation of this powerful ley line.

Denderwindeke, the chapel in the forest

Denderwindeke 9400, Roost
50°48'20.93"N – 3°59'19.07"E

This interesting line continues to the hamlet 'Roost', west of Denderwindeke. A narrow forest path leads to the hilltop to the Saint-Lambert's Chapel from the 16th century. An old report from 1618 describes the chapel having a thatched roof, but also mentioned that it had been attended by no less than 2000 pilgrims in that year. During that period there even were six paths along which one could reach the chapel from different directions.

The chapel is dedicated to the Holy Lambert which was worshipped in order to cure paralysis, fevers and other ailments. Judging from the many ex-votos and arms, legs and heads made from wax, he has accomplished his task well

Along some stairs you reach the adjacent Lambert Well whose water is still used to cure sore eyes and poor visibility. Affected body parts are washed in it, and it is mixed through the food of the animals. In the past, the pilgrims would walk three times around the chapel and three times around the tree that stood next to the well. Afterwards they tied a ribbon or piece of clothing belonging to the sick to a branch of the tree.

The line runs through the interior of the entire chapel and makes it a very quiet and cosy but powerful place worth of visiting.

The hidden by trees Saint Lambert Chapel in the forest of Denderwindeke.

Province Antwerp

From Antwerp to Schelle

It is a strange but also a common view for most of the people living in the south of Antwerp. From the busy road of St. Bernard's (Sint-Bernardsesteenweg) they can see the high tower of the cathedral behind the towers of two other churches. A nice example of a ley line!

Antwerp: Our Lady's Cathedral

Antwerpen 2000, Handschoenmarkt
51°13'12.96"N – 4°24'5.65"E

This Gothic Cathedral with a surface of more than 8000 square meters is the biggest in Belgium and the 123 meter high tower is even the highest

Looking up from the most powerful place in the cathedral.

church tower in Europe. History told there was a little old Roman chapel in the 9th century that was built on the place where a statue of Our Lady was honoured in a tree. This place is situated in the choir of the present cathedral. The building of the cathedral started in 1352 and was completed around 1520, but there were rebuilds until the 16th century. The designers planned to construct five towers as a powerful illustration of the wealth and power of medieval Antwerp, but only one was completed.

Inside, the pentagonal apse and ambulatory with five radiating chapels dates from 1352. The three straight bays of the choir are surrounded by twin side-aisles. The structure was designed by architect Jan Appelmans. A touching monument was erected in his honour outside the cathedral where he taught the stonemasons.

In 1566 and in 1581, during the iconoclastic furies, the interior of the cathedral was badly damaged by the Calvinists. In the 18th century, the French even threatened to demolish the building entirely. Despite the looting that occurred in later centuries, a lot was saved and fabulous paintings by Rubens can still be admired.

We can feel the strong energy below the 43 meter high dome with the beautiful painting 'The Ascension of Mary', and between the painting 'the raising of the Cross' by Peter Paul Rubens and the tabernacle in the form of the Ark of the Covenant in the Sacrament Chapel.

A very powerful ley line runs from here to the southwest over a distance of more than 14 kilometres.

An eighteenth-century watercolor image of the beautiful cathedral.

Church of Saint Andreas (Sint Andrieskerk)

Antwerpen 2000, Sint-Andriesstraat
51°12'59.34"N – 4°23'52.14"E

A few 100 meters further down the line we find the 16th century church dedicated to Saint Andreas; the Sint Andrieskerk. It is here that the monks of Saint Augustine's started a monastery in 1510. Not without some problems, because they preached in the spirit of Luther. In 1522, the monks where banned and the monastery destroyed. A year later the building of the present church started. More important than this turbulent history is the ley line in this beautiful church. Was the line accidentally or deliberately indicated with a star motif in the church floor?

An eight-pointed star motif was purposefully placed where the leyline runs.

Church of Saint Catharina (Sint Catharinakerk)

Antwerpen 2020, Sint-Bernardsesteenweg
51°11'34.99"N – 4°22'46.11"E

The next church can we find on the border of Antwerp. It was built in the 13th century and dedicated to Saint Catharina. It was a very small church so like on many other places, rebuilds followed. The one we find here today dates from 1869 and we find the ley line in the tower. The line runs further down the busy Saint-Bernard's road to the village Hemiksem. According to local history it was a part of the old Roman road between Brussels and Antwerp.

The Sint Bernardsesteenweg with the Saint Catherine church and behind it the tower of the cathedral. The small green dome of the Saint Andreas church is barely visible. A nice example of a ley line.

Abbey of Saint Bernard's (Sint Bernardusabdij)

Hemiksem 2620, Depotstraat
51° 7'53.62"N – 4°19'45.87"E

In Hemiksem, we find the abbey of Saint Bernard's where the old road gets its name from. Founded in 1242, derived from the big abbey of Villers-la-Ville south of Brussels, the place was strategically as spiritually a good choice and became one of the most powerful abbeys of the late middle ages. We can find the ley line in the choir of the abbey church and it is also clearly visible in the surrounding landscape.

Schelle, the Laar Chapel (Laarkapel)

Schelle 2627, Laarhofstraat
51° 7'16.15"N – 4°19'33.95"E

The small 'Laarkapel', a chapel in the next village of Schelle, dates from the 17th century but a lot earlier there stood a chapel on the same place. On the backside we found until a few years back a remarkable block of stone which, according to the legend, would come from Golgotha. Knowing that the surrounding toponyms refer to great stones, this stone possibly was a piece of a megalith.

However, the most recent restoration of the chapel ignores the potential importance of this stone and it disappeared. With 14 kilometres in distance, the ley line ends at a short distance beyond this energetic place.

Antwerp: the calvary of the Saint Paulus Church

Antwerpen 2000, Sint-Paulusstraat
51°13'26.09"N – 4°24'4.96"E

This church was founded on a short but high energetic fault line. This becomes clear when we see the compass pointing the direction of the nave is not facing east, but differs to the south.

From the original monastery that was built here in 1262, not much is left. 'A dark and ugly church that regularly was flooded' says the old chronicle.

In the 16th century, they decided to take it down. The site was raised and a new church was completed in 1535. During the religious wars, it was continually plundered and had several fires to endure. In the last fire in 1968, again a large part of the church was destroyed.

In the early 18th century, a Calvary was built against the southern wall of the church that we can find through a gate at the corner of the Veemarkt and the Zwartzusterstraat. It's a strange garden. A bizarre collection of more than sixty sculptures and bas-reliefs stands on and around the Calvary. In the middle of this unique form of popular piety, runs the so called Angels Way.

The garden was created between 1700 and 1740 on commission of two Dominican brothers and Jerusalem pilgrims who wanted to create a 'Little Jerusalem' here in Antwerp. The main theme of the garden was not only the crucifixion on the Calvary itself; on the contrary, the whole process was shown here.

The Angels Way is flanked on either side by ten angels with passion tools. Left is the garden of the prophets and at the right side we find the four evangelists, Marcus, Lucas, John and Matthew. Even Mary Magdalene, we can find several times in the garden.

Also present, Saint Michaël and his dragon.

On the Calvary itself we see the various scenes of the crucifixion. At the bottom we find the Holy Sepulchre with a beautiful wooden statue of Christ and at the left the purgatory with sinners. On the second floor is Mary Magdalene in a cave with Martha, Lazarus and Saint Michael who defeats the dragon. Above, we find the crucified Christ with a weeping Mary.

The whole environment feels strange but at the same time exudes tranquillity. The divining rod, however, reveals that this complex clearly was constructed following certain energetic properties. A narrow fault line follows the direction of the Angels Way toward the high altar in the church. In the other direction it goes straight to the place where the Walpurgis Church, the first church of the old city, once stood. In 1817 it was demolished, by the straightening of the Scheldt and nothing is left from this ancient shrine. Take your time if you visit the Calvary Garden because it is an attractive place of power that invites to meditation.

An angel shows how this powerful ley line runs. One of the many hidden secrets of the beautiful Saint Paulus church. At the left the high altar.

Ranst, the solstice line of Millegem

Ranst 2520, Sint-Antoniusstraat
51°11'1.36"N – 4°32'44.21"E

The church of Our Lady in Millegem near the village Ranst was mentioned in 1202 but already centuries earlier a church is said to have been here. It is a simple small but charming church in a rural setting.

It was placed on a circular mound with a diameter of about 50 meter which could be the rest of a prehistoric tumulus. The small church is surrounded by trees and against the outside of the chancel is a polyester copy of a 16th century Calvary.

We find here one of the most energetic places of the province of Antwerp because this church is at the hub of several ley lines that converge like the spokes of a wheel. There are straight lines to the village churches of Vremde and Hove, Broechem, Lier and even to the cathedral in Antwerp city.

The line described here is a solstice line running north-east to south-west. This means that an observer at the church of Vremde at midsummer is able to see the sunrise behind the church of Millegem and an observer to the church of Hove would see the sun come up behind the church of Vremde.

On December 21, at the winter solstice when the sun sets in the south-west, an observer at the church of Millegem will see the sun set behind the church of Vremde, the observer in Vremde will see the sun set behind the church of Hove. It is generally known that a number of megaliths often were placed in these directions.

Left the church of Millegem and right, sunset behind the church of Vremde at midwinter.

Narrow footpath between the fields and on the ley line between the churches of Vremde and Millegem.

About 800 meters southwest of the church of Milegem, we find a 300 meter long connection path in the direction of the church of Vremde. In this line it is remarkable that not only the energetic aspect, but also a part of the straight-way theory of Alfred Watkins can be found. Over the entire length of the line we find a higher radiation field than elsewhere in the area and this is also clearly visible in the vegetation.

References to an ancient/ megalithic past of this area we found on old maps with street names like 'Rotschstraat'; Rock Street 'and' Keystraat, which means 'Boulder Street', both referring to large boulders and 'Halfberg' which refers to a small hill or tumulus.

The ley centre or energy field is easy to feel with dowsing rods on the entire surface on which the church was built. It is also interesting to dowse in the surrounding fields, to feel the various ley lines. Also, this location is suited to locate the missing graves on the former cemetery but above all, this special place invites to have a meditation

The church in the next village Vremde is dedicated to Saint John and was built in the 19th century, but old documents of the abbey of Saint Bernard's claims that there already was a church in the 12th century. This means that the current church had several predecessors.

The legend telling how the construction site for the first church was determined and how the village gets his name is interesting.
    'The people that live in a village without a name would build a church. There were different opinions and they could not decide where the church had to come, but the smartest of the village without a name suggested to load a few donkeys with bricks.

They lead the donkeys through the village to an open field. Where the donkeys were put to rest, that would be the building site of the church. After walking around for some time, the donkeys rested in the wettest place in the area where the stones fell off their backs.

That's 'Vremde' (which means 'strange') everybody exclaimed at the same time and immediately the name for the village was also chosen'.

In this context it is not the village name that is important, but where the content of the story originates. However trivial it may seem, the similarity to the history of other village churches is striking.

The third point on this line is the St. Lawrence Church in Hove. Archaeological finds in the environment confirm that Hove was inhabited in the early Iron Age. The present church dates from the 15th century, but the present 12th century baptismal font refers to an ancient Roman church on this site.

Lier; in the footsteps of Saint Gummarus

The history of Lier and adjacent village of Emblem is strongly linked with the legend of the Holy Gummarus, a saint that lived during the early 8th century.

Saint Gummarus and the miracle of the tree on an old image.

He was married with Grimmara, who was known as a woman with a cruel and bad character. When Gummarus had to maintain the order in the Frankish empire, Grimmara made the life of his employees into a real hell. When Gummarus came back in Lier, he was told what terror the people had to endure during his absence. In his attempts to compensate this, he felt the desire to reach God becoming more and more powerful.

The most famous legend of Gummarus tells that he chopped down a large tree in a field along the river Nete. Tormented by the behaviour of Grimmara, the owner came rushing by and accused him of being just as evil as his wife.

However, Gummarus immediately renowned his mistake, sank kneeling in prayer beside the tree and asked for God's help. Afterwards he placed the tree trunk back on its place, took off his girdle and tied it around the trunk where it was cut off.

The first miracle by Gummarus was accomplished; the tree grew further as if nothing had happened. When the landlord saw this miracle, he returned all of Gummarus possessions and recognized him as a holy man. Because of this miracle he became also the patron saint of the city Lier.

In Lier, where the miracle of the tree took place, a first chapel was built around the tree in 1262. According to the legend it stood in the middle of the choir, but when it was threatening to grow through the roof of the church, it was replaced by an iron copy.

The church is also named after the place where the Gummarus hermitage was originally built. A two meters wide ley line runs through the south aisle of the church. To find the underground tunnel between the adjacent monastery and the church is interesting for the dowser. Today, the Kluizekerk (Hermitage church), has been sanctified but the wrought iron tree can still be seen in the Saint Gummarus Church of Lier.

The Saint Pieter's Chapel

Lier 2500, Heilige Geeststraat
51° 7'47.98"N – 4°34'26.53"E

The oldest building of Lier is the Romanesque-Gothic St. Pieter's Chapel, built around 1255. It stands where in 764 a wooden chapel was built by Gummarus. The unknown date of the possibly Celtic images of heads and a serpent above the entrance, suggest that they date from an earlier building on this site. According to legend, Saint Gummarus was buried here, but his body mysteriously disappeared from the grave. His empty tomb is still visible behind the altar. The divining rod shows clearly the course of several water veins and narrow geological faults, which transform the chapel into a very energetic place. A two meter wide fault line runs towards the Saint Gummarus Church across the street.

The entrance of the chapel and the empty grave of Gummarus behind the altar.

The church of Saint Gummarus

Lier 2500, Kardinaal Mercierplein
51° 7'47.98"N – 4°34'26.53"E

In the 13th century, when the old Roman church became too small for the growing population of the city, a new Gothic church was built. After a construction period of more than 200 years, it was finally completed, resulting in a stunning achievement of Brabant Gothic.

The turbulent history of the church learns that different parts were destroyed by lightning and had been affected by the iconoclasm in the 15th

A strange person with glasses, and a double-tailed mermaid on the outside of the church.

Saint George slaying the dragon with Maria Magdalena next to him.

and 16th centuries. Miraculously, the stained glass windows where saved. The exterior has a wealth of gargoyles, mythical creatures, satyrs, angels and dragons. Particularly striking are the bespectacled heads, quite unusual in a 14th century tower. The dragon slayer Saint George, the conqueror of the earth energy, can be found on the right side of the entrance, and a double-tailed mermaid, the symbol of the feminine energy on the left.

Beyond the energetic aspect of this impressive church, it is worth to detect the different water veins with dowsing rods. Several veins can be found around the altar and in the vicinity of the iron tree. The many old gravestones on the undulating floor level show clearly the unstable soil.

Although the church is filled with many gorgeous sculptures, the austere St. George's Chapel is the most powerful place of the whole church. A ley line runs from here to the shrine where the bones of Holy Gummarus have been

Left; the interior of the church and right; the heavy shrine is carried trough the streets during the procession.

stored. It is located behind a diptych that suggests the miracle of the tree and is exhibited only once a year, during the Saint Gummarus celebration.

Annually, on the first Sunday after October 10th, a procession is held, in which the more than 800 kilogram shrine is worn by sixteen men through the streets of Lier. After the Holy Mass on that day, the priest puts the girdle of Gummarus, a symbolic copy of the one which performed the miracle of the tree, on the shoulders of the pilgrim. This blessing is done, not only to ask for healing the fractured bones, but also in difficult marital situations that sometimes could lead to a breakup.

Emblem, the Gummarus Chapel

Emblem 2520, Dorpstraat
51° 9'40.15"N – 4°36'0.33"E

The baroque Saint Gummarus chapel dates from the 15th century. According to the legend, on a sweltering hot day Gummarus would do something to quench the thirst of his labourers. No need to get a drink, he planted his

The Gummarus Chapel, on the backside leads a stair to the spring.

staff into the ground and immediately a fresh source sprang. Everyone was convinced that this work was divine, because the water tasted better than the best wine.

After the many miracles that took place, a first chapel was built on top of the source. This chapel was already mentioned in the 11th century but also was destroyed several times by lightning.

The plants in the vicinity show that the vegetation clearly was inhibited by the influence of the strong ley line. The trees next to the chapel also suffered from the strong radiation field, so regularly new ones should be planted.

The line runs further into the new 19th century church of Emblem. According to legend, it was built under his insurance as the cemetery of Gummarus, but another legend sited his tomb in Saint Peter's Chapel in the centre of Lier. We find the five meters wide ley line in the left aisle of the church.

Geel; the church of Saint Dimpna

Geel 2440, Sint Dimpnaplein
51° 9'45.40"N – 5° 0'6.22"E

The history of the city of Geel is directly linked to the legend of the Holy Dimpna. The story dates from the 13th century, tells that she was a pagan and according to later sources, the daughter of an Irish king, who after the death of his wife wanted to force Dimpna to marry him. Together with her protector, father Gerebernus she could escape from Ireland until they finally landed in Geel. After a long search her father had finally found her. Gerebernus was killed by his soldiers and Dimpna beheaded by her own father.

On this place the Gothic church of Geel was built. The construction was started in 1350, but it would take almost 200 years before it was completed. The church was badly damaged during the Second World War, but later fully constructed. Fine gargoyles look down from the walls of the old church on the side of the cemetery.

Inside we find a range of treasures, but the most important is a shrine containing the coffins with the remains of Dimpna and Gerebernus. Several miraculous cures were attributed to her. For centuries there was a busy pilgrimage to her relics. Dimpna mainly was invoked against mental illness. From all over the area, sick people came to Geel where they did a nine days novena.

The community provided them shelter for the duration of the pilgrimage and from this grew the home health care which still is known at this they and age.

Saint Dimpna kills the dragon at the gate of the church and one of the strange gargoyles on the tower.

A powerful ley line runs through the cemetery to the oldest part of the church.

The curious legend of Saint Dimpna is accompanied by a highly energetic ley line. We find it central to the church and running further east to the Chapel of the Green Hill (kapel van de Groene Heuvel). According to the ancient history, pilgrims had robbed the relics of Saint Dimpna and Gerebernus. Chased by the angry residents they had to leave the boxes behind on this place. To commemorate this fact, the chapel was built.

Zammel, the Chapel of Saint Dimpna

Zammel 2440, Sint-Gerebernusstraat
51° 6'1.50"N – 4°57'35.42"E

Zammel, a small village south of Geel, plays also an important role in the history of the city. The Holy Dimpna Chapel with its source is overshadowed by an ancient lime tree. According to legend, Dimpna lived here in a hermitage before she was found and murdered by her father. Since the Middle Ages pilgrims came to this place for the healing properties of the water.

A source, a tree and a chapel possibly replacing megaliths? The Pagan elements in this chapel still exist. The highly energetic atmosphere of this place invites to engage in meditation.

The small but highly energetic chapel with lime tree and source.

Province Flemish Brabant

Scherpenheuvel, from Holy Tree to Basilica

Scherpenheuvel 3270, Basilieklaan
50°58'49.09"N – 4°58'40.42"E

With over one million visitors annually, the Basilica of Scherpenheuvel is the most famous Pilgrimage site in Flanders. Every year in the month of May, groups of pilgrims from all directions walk to this sanctuary, coming from sometimes thirty to forty kilometres away. The most famous pilgrimage starting from the city of Antwerp is 57 km long. Others prefer to take part by bike or by car. What draws these people to this place? However, the legend preceding the creation of this sanctuary sounds familiar.

The Basilica of Scherpenheuvel is a typical example of pagan worship of a sacred oak was able to develop into a popular Christian pilgrimage site. It is the familiar form of the way tree devotion was Christianized by putting a statue of the Madonna in the tree. We can find such examples by the dozen in Flanders.

In a 14th century chronicle we read that in 1304 a sacred oak containing a statue with miraculous powers was revered on this hill. Later, the place got well known because of an incident that took place in 1415. A shepherd who left his flock to graze at the foot of the sacred oak saw that the Madonna statue had fallen from the tree. He picked it up with the intention to take it home, but that did him no good. He remained as if nailed to the ground, unable to move any longer.

Because he did not appear on the farm that evening, it was decided to search for him. They found the shepherd like frozen with the statue in his hands, but as it was placed back into the tree; the poor man was released and regained his forces. Like on many other sites this was a sign for the Blessed Virgin to be venerated on her 'Sharp Hill'.

A first chapel was built next to the tree in 1602 and a first really miraculous healing dates back to May of that same year. A young blind girl got her sight back after she had washed her eyes with water from the nearby well. This 90 meters deep pit is still located next to the basilica.

When on January 3 in 1603, the aldermen of the surrounding villages visited the Mary Chapel, a miracle happens. After a short prayer suddenly a drop of blood appears on the lips of the statue. The news spreads like fire throughout the valley and soon people came from all over the country to take part in a pilgrimage to Scherpenheuvel.

That year, the Archbishop gave the order to chop down the tree because of the continued worship and the superstitions still taking place. Already over 49 miraculous healings had been recorded, so the rush was increasing. The believers did engage in the procession to the statue, but continued to worship the tree and pieces of bark and twigs were taken as relics. That same year, there were over twenty thousand pilgrims. The plague which made countless victims during this period has probably contributed to the commotion.

A stone chapel replaced the wooden, until in 1609 the Archdukes Albert and Isabella of Austria gave instructions to build the giant basilica. It was placed

The basilica with 298 seven-pointed gold stars on the dome and the sacred oak above the altar.

in the centre of a seven pointed star floor plan, with the altar on the same place where the sacred oak once stood.

The construction took more than twenty years for the imposing structure to complete. The seven-part high central dome, set with 298 seven-pointed gold stars, symbolized the reflection of the cosmos. With the creation of the dome, it was as if the sky had been taken down. Here, in essence, the cosmic and earthly energies got united. Also the magical number seven can be found several times in the basilica.

In the basilica, there are seven chapels and seven paintings depicting the life of Mary, we even find seven medallions in each stained glass window. The centre of the church's main altar leans against one of the seven pillars that support the dome.

The many votive offerings refer to the remarkable number of healings that took place here. The powerful energy of this sanctuary can be felt from a distance. From the heptagonal park, seven ways follow seven ley lines in different directions.

Laken: two churches and a fountain

Laken 1020, Sint Annadreef
50°52'43.84"N – 4°21'20.61"E and 50°53'14.93"N – 4°21'9.64"E

The pilgrimage to the church and the fountain of Our Lady of Laken was, in the past, one of the most famous of Belgium. History tells us that in the year 900 two sisters decided to build a small chapel for Mary. When the chapel was completed, it soon became a place where many sick were healed after they had prayed to the statue of the Holy Virgin.

In the 13th century, forced by the many visitors, a larger church was build, but the buildings were destroyed three times during consecutive nights. On the fourth night, the Holy Virgin appeared and told that a plan for the new church would be offered.

'Here is a thread that indicates the size of the church', she said. 'The church must be directed towards Brussels, and I shall protect my sanctuary and my son himself will come to consecrate the church.' According to the legend, the church was indeed consecrated by Jesus himself on Easter Day, accompanied by his mother and a choir of singing angels.

Dragons everywhere in and outside the old church. During our visit, a cat takes some rest on the very powerful ley line.

Pilgrims came rushing in from all directions to worship the miraculous statue of Our Lady. During the Religious War, a big part of the church was destroyed by the Calvinists. Strict Catholic Archdukes Albert and Isabella (1595-1633) had the church restored and the miraculous Madonna that had been hidden in the convent of Brussels, returned to Laken.

Today, the choir is the only surviving remainder from the old church that was demolished in the early 20th century. It stands in the middle of the historic cemetery. The whole of the outside and inside is decorated with dragons, not without reason. It is still a very powerful place. 50°52'47.11"N – 4°21'16.97"E

From here, a ley line runs from the spot the Infant Isabella commanded a new avenue instead of the old road north of the church, in the direction of the miraculous source a few hundred meters to the north. A Latin inscription near the source reminds us of that gift.

Traditionally, the water had miraculous and curative powers against fever, cramps and other illnesses, and the source was for centuries a place of pilgrimage. The Saint Anne source was also called 'The Fountain of the Five Wounds' because the water flowed out of five holes, and symbolized the wounds of Christ. Behind the source Isabella built a chapel which was dedicated to Saint Anne.

On the other side of the cemetery we find the new church dating from 1854. There the foundation stone was laid by King Leopold I. The two precious

The very dilapidated Fountain of the Five Wounds with the Saint Anna Chapel behind.

relics, the miraculous statue and the wonderful wire emerge at the Holy Virgin site of the old church and were transferred to the new church. Since then, the crypt of the church serves as a tomb for the royal family.

On the outside we also find many dragon-slayer saints. Again a reference to the powerful energy line on which this church, the source and the old church on the cemetery was built. From here, the ley line runs further to the well know Saint Michael's Cathedral in Brussels.

A small selection of the many dragon slayers on the outside of the new church.

Halle and its Black Madonna

Halle 1500, Grote Markt
50°44'12.06"N – 4°14'14.11"E

The basilica of Halle is located in the centre of the city and was built in the 14th century to replace an old oratory of Saint Martin. It is even not described, but everything points out that pagan tree worship took place here, before the Black Madonna statue was worshipped. The ultimate proof we can still find in the floor of the crypt. During restoration at the beginning of the previous century, it was discovered that the original floor was missing some tiles. Great was the surprise when an old tree stump was carefully preserved in the floor.

But this building has much more to hide. The basilica is oriented to the northeast, the point where the sun rises on June 21 during the summer solstice. Not that evident, as in this period practically all the churches were build facing east.

The whole building is steeped with pagan symbols found either inside or outside. Before entering the church we are welcomed by hundreds of spirits of nature. The two old oak doors of the south portal are decorated with twisted wrought iron whose ends portray acorns and oak leaves. Each of these oak leaves has its own little

Little faces on the oak leaves of the entrance door. Inside the church; Wodan with his messengers and a bishop with donkey ears.

face; the green men from the old nature devotion are welcoming you here very clearly. We will find it hidden almost everywhere in the church even in the keystone of the tower.

The inside as well as the outside is richly provided with sculpted consoles and corbels. The basilica has more than 150 weird sculptures clearly carved by stonemasons with still a pagan nature. Dragons spy on us around the choir from all angles and sides. A bishop was depicted with donkey ears, a unicorn is ridden by an angel and even Wodan, the great god of the Old Germanics is shown here with his usual companions, the ravens Hugin and Munin, symbols of intelligence and memory.

But Halle is best known as the Basilica with its miraculous Black Madonna, a statue that was donated by Aleydis of Avesnes, wife of the Duke of Hennegau to the old St. Martin's church in 1267. Her most important miracle was the resurrection of stillborn infants, the time needed to get baptized. If not baptized, their soul couldn't go to heaven.

Her presence transformed the church into a pilgrimage place and people came from far to visit her. The statue is still annually honoured by ten thousands of pilgrims and no fewer than 129 miracles have been attributed.

Black Madonna's; with their mysterious aura have always posed a dilemma to the church. Sometimes they are completely black, but often they have only a black face, or black hands and feet. Various explanations

Burning a candle for the Black Madonna and the old tree stump carefully preserved in the floor of the crypt.

of the origin of the dark colour followed each other over the centuries. They were cut out of dark wood, the silver paint with which they were painted had been oxidized, or they would have had their dark colour from the candle smoke. The Black Madonna of Halle is said to have been blackened from the smoke of the cannonballs which she received in her lap during the siege of the city in 1489! The blockade was therefore abandoned. In a recess under the tower we find the famous 32 cannon balls and a stone from the ancient fortress wall reminds us of this incident.

Mostly, the statues of the black Mother Goddess originated from the Celtic period and display the Goddess of nature. Sometimes they were found to next to Holy Wells, in a cave or buried in the ground to indicate the holiness of that place. The familiar black Notre-Dame-sous-Terre (Our Lady of the underworld) in Chartres is a striking example. Not without reason the cathedral was built on this particular site.

Elsewhere in Europe, Black Madonna's have always been an object of profound veneration, because they possessed the ability to make barren women fertile. Especially famous for several miracles is the Black Virgin of Guadalupe in Spain. Both Columbus and Cortes made a pilgrimage to the cave where she still is, before sailing to America. Everywhere, churches with a Black Madonna grew into well-known pilgrimage places.

The church also keeps an ancient tradition very much alive. In the Chapel of Our Lady lies the grave of the little Joachim, the deceased son of the French Dauphin, Louis XI and Charlotte of Savoy. Dating from 1459, it was stored in a lead casket and buried under a grey marble slab.
    The birth had been announced from Halle by Louis, but four months later the baby died and was buried in the church.
    Stroking the tummy of the small figure lying at the entrance of the choir was said to bring good luck, and was an act of the pilgrims before beginning their tour around the altar. Possibly this was also a fertility rite, as the Black Madonna was mainly visited to obtain a fruitful marriage. Not without reason, therefore, Princess Mathilde donated her bridal bouquet to the church of Halle, after she married. The result is well known.

The implantation of the Church points to several faults, some of which are still followed by the pilgrims. West of the city we can find a five kilometres long procession road. Several factors suggest that this procession originates from pagan times. According to historians, this processional way is related to the old Goddess Hella. The footpaths through the fields are flanked by 43 chapels of various shapes and age. For those wanting to experience the energetic aspect of the environment, this pilgrimage comes highly recommended.

Stroking the tummy of the little Joachim would bring good luck.

From Hakendover to Grimde

Hakendover 3300, Hakendoverstraat
50°47'39.18"N – 4°58'53.18"E

The 12th century church of Hakendover with her Romanesque tower stands on a hill. Beside the church, we find a hawthorn which is closely linked with the construction history of the church.

The legend tells us that in the year 690 three ladies decided to build a church for the Holy Saviour. This was not so easy, because what was built during the day was destroyed at night by the devil. The desperate virgins started praying and asked the advice of God. But suddenly, an angel appeared and guided the ladies through the snow to a place called the 'Steenberg', the Stone Hill. Here they found a blooming hawthorn in a place that was without any snow.

The angel ordered that the church must be built by twelve workmen. Whatever happened, twelve people were told, twelve appeared at lunch at the table and twelve got paid. But while the works go on, there were always thirteen bricklayers counted. Once the church was completed, the thirteenth worker was recognised as the Lord himself.

The annual procession which takes place during the night of 16th on 17th January has mentioned 'thirteen times'. It consists of a pilgrimage going thirteen times up and down from the Church of the Divine Saviour in Hakendover to the Our Lady of the Stone Chapel in the village of Grimde.
It follows a part of the ancient Roman road that connects the two sanctuaries. Also on Easter Monday, pilgrims and riders from all over the country go to Hakendover, to attend the horse procession.

After the blessing of the pilgrims in the open field, the riders would trot three times around the altar. Then, according to ancient tradition, several hundred horses galloping over the fields to awaken the earth after the long winter.

The church of Hakendover.

At the foot of the Church Hill in Hakendover we find the Saint Salvator Well with holy water. Next to the church stands the Holy Thorn where pilgrims cut twigs to take home and further, a loft with holy earth to prevent all kinds of mischief and to promote fertility. This set of magical objects and actions are clearly not Christian, but originated from Celtic or Germanic origin. The name 'Steenberg', Stone Hill, suggests that originally, megaliths stood on this hill.

A few kilometres from Hakendover the Chapel of Our Lady of the Stone (O.L.Vrouw ten Steen Kapel) is situated. 50°47'55.40"N – 4°57'49.76"E.

The chapel takes us through different construction periods to arrive at the era of the megalith builders. By reconstructing the street and square, there is unfortunately little evidence left of the two remaining small standing stones which stand next to the chapel. History tells us that the chapel was founded in 1325 and dedicated to Saint Maurus. A pilgrimage to the chapel, cured the most severe headache when one of the metal crowns was put on one's head.

The front and backside of the chapel with the small standing stone. Right, the altar of St. Maurus and the metal crowns which would cure the worst headache.

A few hundred meters further, three Roman tumuli are to be found in a straight line with the chapel and the church of Hakendover. Burial mounds were also put on an energetic place to give the dead the necessary energy for their journey through the afterlife. This ley line runs further into the Saint Peter's Church of Grimde.

A next step on the line in the direction of Tienen brings us to the place where in the past the 'Lion's Rock' stood. An old engraving shows a large, heavily leaning standing stone. If the human proportions are correct, this should have been a gigantesque stone of ten meters high. Around 1837 it is said to have been destroyed or buried during the construction of the railway, but a correct location is uncertain.

The vanished large standing stone.

Province Limburg

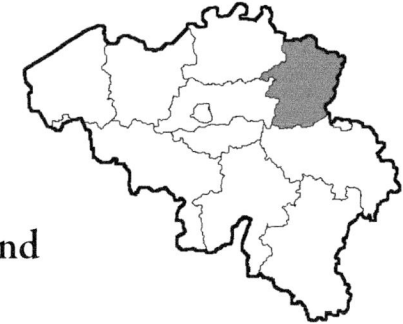

Rutten: the Sacred Meadow and the chapel of Evermarus

Rutten 3700, Motstraat
50°44'42.36"N – 5°26'41.02"E

It was during the 7th century that Evermarus and his seven companions took a break after their pilgrimage to Santiago de Compostela. But it would be fatal, because in this meadow they were killed by a gang of robbers. Their bodies were found at night by hunters who saw the body of Evermarus shine as a ray of light in the dark. Because this happens only by Holy martyrs, the people of Rutten are said to have built a chapel on the place where he died.

According to legend, two deer appeared suddenly and gave instructions to the people of Rutten to commemorate Evermarus annually on the first of May in a mystery play. However, the bishop refused to consecrate the chapel because he found the story to be unbelievable. Anyway, a first chapel was built in 1073 on the site of a wooden church which was founded on the place of a Roman temple. Possibly this temple replaced a megalithic structure.

On this strange place we find besides a Chapel, also a well and a circle of trees. For centuries, the people of Rutten had been aware, that the soil of this place had a very strong force. In the floor of the chapel is a pit where even today sand is being scooped by the locals to mix it in the food of their animals. Sick animals are said to be healed by this practice.

The nearby source would possess healing water. The water vein, on which the source is located, runs to the north towards Saint Martin's Church a few hundred meters further. The energetic aspect of this place is to be found all around the Sacred Meadow. The tree circle with eight limes, symbolizes Evermarus and his seven companions. It would not be surprising that this was originally the site of a stone circle.

The Sacred Meadow in Rutten; with source, tree circle and the chapel in the background.

Interesting, is the Evermarus play that was ordered by two talking deer is celebrated every year on the first of May, the Celtic Beltane. This proves that on this place we find all the elements that refer to a pre-Christian shrine. By our ancestors, the deer was seen as the bearer of the soul of the forest. The role the deer play in the passion play, clearly referring to the ancient nature religions of the Celts. In the play there also are two men who wear a hat of ivy and a club. These figures are well known as the 'green man' or 'Jack-in-the-green'. By wearing leafs and deer antlers they symbolized the fertility of nature and came in contact with the natural spirits. Finally in this play, there are the horsemen galloping during the play of the Sacred Meadow. It is an ancient spring ritual that aims to awaken the earth after the long hibernation.

The Holy House of Herstappe

Herstappe 3717, Luykerweg
50°43'42.06"N – 5°26'0.14"E

Herstappe, the smallest village of Flanders is located between Tongeren and Heers. Barely one square kilometre, there are two streets and a handful of houses around the church. It forms a fabulous walking field with meadows, acres, clean air and a fascinating history.

A few hundred yards past the church you will find a hollow way which leads to the Holy House, a desolate chapel flanked by two lime trees. No, we are not in Flanders anymore, but only a few meters across the language border.

An information board tells us that the chapel was erected to commemorate the bloody battle of 1408 when Duke John of Brabant, also known as John the Fearless, defeated here 6000 citizens of Liege. This is very well possible of course but it is not really known when the chapel was built. The year 1719, which was engraved above the door, refers not to the construction date, but to the year it was restored.

The Chapel between two lime trees.

Nine church towers are visible from here and around the chapel; six ley lines can be found with the divining rod. The chapel forms a strong leycentre towards the Basilica of Tongeren and the churches of Rutten, Diets-Heur and Lauw in Flanders, and Othée, Crisnée and Villers-l'Eveque in Wallonnia. One line runs through the Herstappe tomb, a Roman tumulus.

Kuringen: the Abbey of Herkenrode

Kuringen 3511, Herkenrodeabdij
50°57'21.30"N – 5°16'43.45"E

A statue of a unicorn welcomes visitors to the abbey of Herkenrode. In the yard we find multiple times its effigy. What is the purpose of this mythical animal? Is the unicorn just a reference to the mystical symbolism of the Christian iconography that suggests the chastity of the Immaculate Virgin, or is there more? The abbey bears also a unicorn in her arms which is very strange because it is a mythical animal. Usually we find in the arms of abbeys an image of an animal that can be linked directly with the environment.

Thus, the abbey of St. Bernard's on the Scheldt in Hemiksem (Province of Antwerp) has a heron in its arms. Given its location on the banks of the Scheldt, it was a common animal here. The great Abbey of Villers la Ville, located in the forests of Brabant had a falcon, the Abbey on the Dunes in Koksijde in West Flanders a fish. Always images of animals from the neighbourhood, never mythical creatures.

In heraldry the unicorn stands for his fighting spirit and bravery. For centuries several towns, nobility and religious orders used shields to prove their identity. The best known example is that where the unicorn stands together with a lion in the arms of the United Kingdom. Their relationship originated from the story that the lion would be the only animal ever to be mastered by the unicorn.

Unicorns everywhere in the abbey of Herkenrode.

However, does the link between the abbey and the unicorn due to fiction in the strange legend explain the origin of the abbey? In 1182 Count Gerard van Loon is said to have been hunting in the forests of Herkenrode when he found three maidens on the banks of a river in the company of a unicorn. They told the inquisitive Count they had taken distance from the worldly life, and wanted to spend the rest of their lives in prayer and seclusion to devote the Lord. The devout Count immediately gave them a piece of his 3000 acres property to build an abbey. Ingeltrude, the oldest of the three maidens became the first abbess of Herkenrode and also chose the arms of the abbey with the leaping unicorn. Therefore, the Abbey became the first Cistercian abbey for women in Belgium.

On the abbey property run several ley lines. As in most monasteries they were aware of the most energetic places during the building process and those were therefore fully exploited. Like in most abbeys we also find in Herkenrode a powerful ley line in the cloister were the prayers took place, and in the church.

The Holstones of Zonhoven

Zonhoven 3520, Holsteenweg
50°59'45.29"N – 5°25'1.27"E

In Zonhoven is a complex of eight huge blocks of stone, partly half under and half above ground. The blocks are composed of quartz-rich sea sand, formed in the Late Miocene (26 to 5 million years ago) a time when all of Flanders was situated below sea-level.

In the past, the locals considered the ancient mystical stones as the so called 'Alvermannekes' little nature spirits. There was also the tempting idea that the stones were once part of a megalithic complex, and even a comparison with Stonehenge was made.

The strange shaped Holstones on a powerful ley line.

Currently, archaeologists are convinced that the blocks were prehistoric grinding wheels. The unusual form was indeed explained by the geological conditions, but most cuts and joints were the result of grinding and polishing stones to sharp objects.

The confirmation for this comes from various archaeological excavations in the area where different sites from the Old and New Stone Age were found.

Although it concerns a natural rock formation, the energetic aspect is clearly noticeable. The compass shows that the geomagnetic field is clearly disturbed here. A very strange place!

Wallonia

Province Walloon Brabant

The abbey of Villers-la-Ville

Villers-La-Ville 1495, Rue de l'Abbaye
50°35'26.31"N – 4°31'46.73"E

With her majestic ruins, imposing vaulted roofs, arches and rose windows Villers-la-Ville is without doubt Belgium's most visited abbey. Founded in 1146 by Bernard of Clervaux, it was the major spiritual centre of Northern Europe.

The history of the Abbey dates back to the 12th century, although most of the ruins are from at least one century later. Deterioration of the abbey started in the 16th and 17th century. Despite being ravaged and laid waste several times over the centuries by the Spanish in 1544 and the French in 1796, it was continually restored by the faithful.

Although in the 18th century the abbey flourishes during a second golden period until in 1796 the French Revolution occurs, during which the monastery was destroyed, abandoned, then plundered and used as a quarry for nearby stone buildings.

With up to 100 monks and 300 lay brothers residing within its grey stone walls, the monastery estate ranged out over 25,000 acres at its heyday in the 13th century. Today, strolling through the ruins you get a touching look at how the monks lived and worshipped as you walk through the abbey. The abbey was almost a small city where the monks and lay brothers worked in silence, forging steel in the foundry, doing laundry and caring for the animals in the stable.

It's impossible not to be fascinated by the Romanesque and Gothic chapel walls and through the medieval arches leading to nowhere, with collapsed round columns lying strewn around you.

You can still feel the haunted atmosphere of these deserted ruins when you walk between the ever-present ivy covered walls. The stained glass windows in the tall arched windows, and smaller round and arched gothic windows must have looked spectacular as light shone in through them.

When you walk through this wonderful abbey, try to 'listen' with your heart, as the Holy Benedict instructed. Spend the time you destine to your hikes in silence, waiting to hear what each place had to say and you will never forget the moment that this abbey enchanted you. Also in this abbey there are several ley lines and you shall feel them, even without dowsing rods. The St. Bernard's Chapel, the cloister and almost the whole church are still very powerful places.

Province Namur

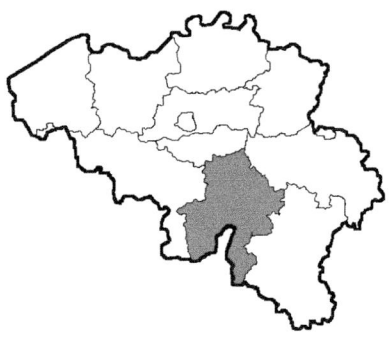

The megaliths of Saint Mort

Haillot 5351, Rue Saint-Mort
50°27'38.61"N – 5° 8'39.50"E

In the vicinity of Andenne a local saint with the strange name 'Mort' was being honoured. He was a hermit that lived in the 7th century in the forests of Haillot. The legend tells how the hermit was given his strange name.

'A woman became aware that the child she bore in her womb was dead. She went to the church in Huy where a miraculous Black Madonna was being worshipped, the protector of stillborn children. Once there, the woman gave birth to her dead son on the altar before she sank in prayer. A miracle

The small standing stone beneath the altar.

occurred, the child was alive. The mother called her son Mort, because he had been raised from the dead.'

Mort became a swineherd to the Holy Begga and lived secluded in the woods between the ancient megaliths. He died at the age of eighty years old and would probably have become much older, if it had not been for the fact that he was murdered by a gang of robbers.

The inhabitants of Andenne, by whom Mort was much loved, wanted to bury the hermit in their city. He was a laid on a cart but the horses refused to move one leg. The people saw this as the intervention of divine intervention and decided to let the horses go. They ran to Huy all by themselves and stopped at the church where Mort was stillborn into the world. The hermit was buried in the church and declared holy.

A few hundred meters from the Saint Mort Chapel stands the Devil's Stone also Christianised with a chapel.

The legend goes on and tells that Mort died at a megalith. The stone, on which he died, probably the capstone of a dolmen, now covers his tomb in the church of Huy that had been commanded for him. The church was visited frequently in the past, and many pilgrims put gifts on the tombstone. With a spoon available, stone powder was scraped from the tombstone and mixed with food or drink for its curative or healing properties. The Black Madonna, that had awakened the dead born Mort to life, has now vanished.

But also in the 15th century Chapel of Saint Mort in Haillot is still a megalith. It sits under the altar, and only the top part is visible. It has never been studied how deep it actually is below the ground. On the altar we find the text: 'L'an 613 de ce lieu St. MORT mounting aux Cieux' (in the year 613 St. Mort rose to heaven from this spot).

Pilgrims came to the chapel to get rid of headaches, neck pain, dental pain or kidney stones. They had to kneel before the altar and then kiss the top of the stone. To complete and to succeed the ritual it was necessary to walk from the chapel to the tomb of St. Mort in Huy.

The earth around the megalith is sacred, taken home and mixed with the food of the animals. Cows were believed to give more milk and therefore remain free of disease. This clearly points out the knowledge of the power of this place. The other megaliths in the area can only be discovered with difficulty. Along a track we find a single stone that is called the 'Devil's Stone' and was converted into a Christian Chapel.

THE MEGALITHS OF WERIS

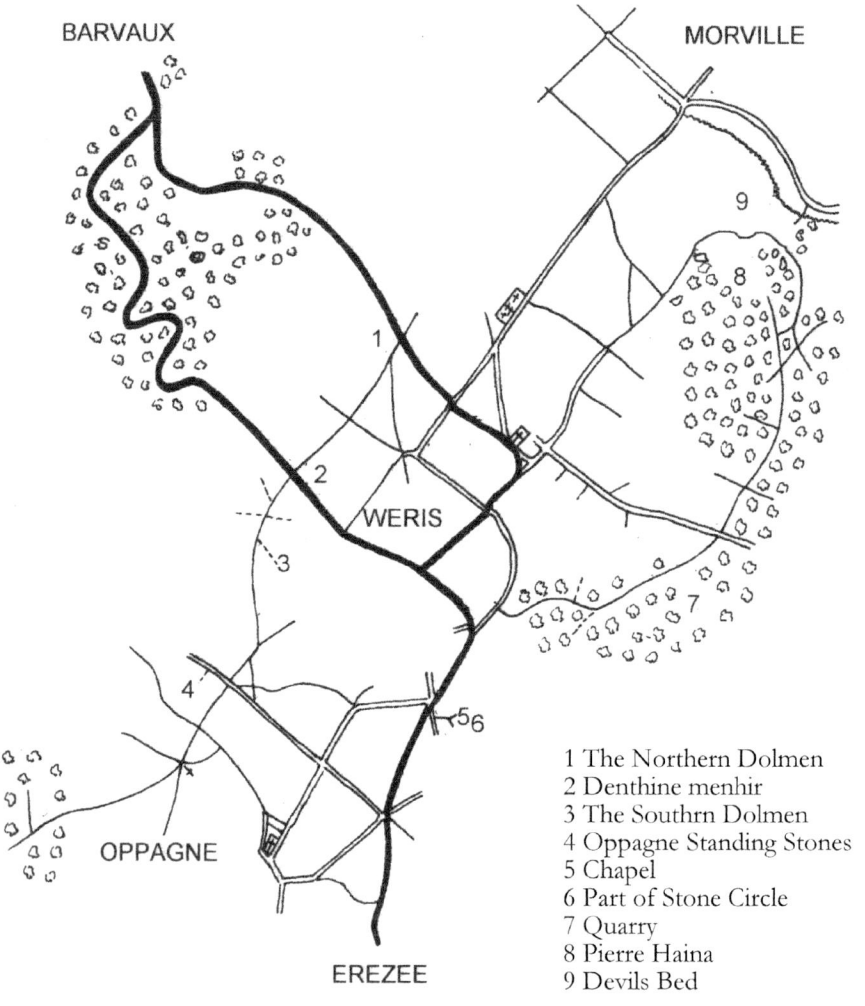

1 The Northern Dolmen
2 Denthine menhir
3 The Southrn Dolmen
4 Oppagne Standing Stones
5 Chapel
6 Part of Stone Circle
7 Quarry
8 Pierre Haina
9 Devils Bed

Province Luxembourg

The megaliths of Weris

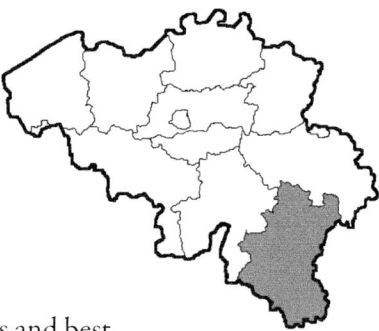

The megaliths of Weris are the most famous and best preserved in Belgium. They were erected by the so called Seine-Oise-Marne culture that emerged around 3000 BC in Northern France. All megaliths are made of the so called 'pudding stone', a conglomerate of quartzite and sandstone held together by a binder of small pebbles. This composition makes those stones look like a kind of natural concrete.

The Northern Dolmen

Weris 6940, Rue des dolmens
50°19'59.97"N – 5°31'21.67"E

The northern dolmen was named that way because of its geographical location and is situated along the road from Weris to Barvaux. In 1882, the

Belgian State bought the monument for the sum of 1,200 Belgian francs (30 Euros).

The first excavations took place in 1888, but real archaeological research began around 1980 by the National Service for Excavations. The dolmen is north – east oriented and is 10 meters long. On top we find two large capstones. The largest measuring 4.75 to 3.60 meter and weighs about 30 tons. In 1984, a number of stone blocks was found in the field next to the dolmen and placed before the entrance.

This is the same field where in 1947 the Danthine-menhir was discovered during ploughing. It was re-established in 1947 by Helene Danthine, an archaeologist at the University of Liege. At the request of the farmer this was not done on his land, but at the edge of the field along the road to Barvaux-Erezée. The standing stone is 3.60 meters tall and weighs about 8 tons.

The Southern Dolmen

Weris 6940
50°19'17.77"N – 5°30'46.95"E

Protected by four ancient oaks serving as guards, lies the dolmen of Oppagne, also called the southern dolmen, somewhat hidden in the soil. It was also

discovered by a farmer while ploughing in 1888. The dolmen has almost the same structure as the northern dolmen, consists of thirteen stones and is six meters long. That this dolmen actually has been used as a burial chamber was proved by the discovery of nine skeletons. Both dolmens are equipped with a stone with a circular hole called 'a hole for the soul' by the archaeologists. This hole made it possible for the soul of the deceased to escape from the burial chamber.

Archaeological investigation has also revealed some flint stone pins and sand potsherds. East of the dolmen, stand the five standing stones that were discovered during excavations in 1986 and 1997.

The menhirs of Oppagne

50°19'2.36"N – 5°30'31.48"E

In the territory of Oppagne three standing stones are situated in a field next to a pear tree. They were excavated in 1906 and have been put upright without further examination. Short after World War II, a hotel owner from Hotton relocated the stones to the garden of his hotel as some sort of curiosity. The government, however, forced him to put the stones back, but during this operation one of the stones broke. It is therefore unclear whether originally there were two or three stones.

The Pierre Haina

50°19'59.64"N – 5°32'34.57"E

The white Pierre Haina is located on a hill and is visible from afar in the surrounding area. It is not a standing stone, but a three meters high carved rock pillar. The origin and meaning of its strange name is unsure. Possibly the word is Celtic and means 'the Stone of the Ancestors'.

In the past, traditionally, the inhabitants of Weris painted the rock white during midsummer and then celebrated the summer solstice on the underlying platform.

The whitewashing clearly was intended to be visible from afar, which certainly must have been the case when the sun was shining. Possibly it served as a beacon to indicate the nearby sacral place for celebrations. According to the legend the Pierre Haina closes an underground corridor which leads to hell.

Devils Bed (Lit du Diable)

50°20'6.02"N – 5°32'35.15"E

Sometimes the devil appeared to perform some evil, and afterwards he went to rest at the nearby 'Lit du Diable' or the Devils Bed. Another story points out that Satan chose the place for the nearby witches to perform their rituals on Walpurgis Night.

The 'Lit du Diable' at the foot of the hill is a piece of rock about 2.45 meters long and 1.45 meters wide. Located on a very energetic place it could be a fallen standing stone, but some think it was a sacrificial table. Because of its strange shape the stone looks like a bed of which the pillow is on the high end. The top seems hollow and shines like a polished stone.

The Saint Walburgis church

50°19'35.54"N – 5°31'49.63"E

The village church of Weris dates from the 11th century and is partially in Romanesque style. It stands in the middle of the former churchyard grounds and is dedicated to Saint Walburgis. Both this church and the church of Tohogne belong to the eldest in the region. Why this saint was chosen is unknown, but Walburgis or Walburga is celebrated on the first of May, also the date of Beltane an important Celtic annual festival.

The night of April 30 to May 1st is also known as the night of Walburgis and as the night of black magic. Witches then held their big meeting which was dominated by the worship of feminine and masculine forces of nature.

Ley lines in Weris
The Belgian orthodox archaeologists still reject the existence of ley lines, but in Weris they are confronted with a real phenomenon. It has been noted that several of the megaliths over a distance of almost eight kilometres are standing in a straight line. The line runs northeast – southwest and consists of three Standing Stones of Oppagne, the Southern Dolmen, the Danthine Menhir, the Northern Dolmen, a small Standing Stone in Morville and the menhir of Heyd which was discovered in 1995. A real gift to ley line-enthusiasts!

The standing stone of Ozo

50°22'47.10"N – 5°33'56.46"E

The menhir of Ozo is 3.40 meter high and weighs 6.5 tons. It was discovered in 1995 and put right back on the same place. Noteworthy is its exact place in between the churches of Ozo and Izier, so we can conclude that this stone may have had an astronomical function. The high tower of the Saint Germain Church in Izier is visible from far and is exactly northeast of the menhir of Ozo. Although the present church was built in the 19th century to replace an older church, it is quite possible that there was a high standing stone in the past.

The standing stone of Ozo with the church tower of Izier in the distance.

Izier was once known for its many wells, but became more famous in the 16th century, when the village tasted the bitter consequences of the witch persecution. History tells us that a woman by the name of Anne Bertrand was accused of participating in nightly dancing with the devil in Werbomont. She was arrested; all her assets were confiscated and evidence was being gathered against her. She was accused of killing a child, the loss of cattle and of poisoning several residents of the village. Anne denied being a witch, but two witches from Hamoir, who had been sentenced to dead, testified against her. When she finally admitted, she was tortured and bound at a brick pile, probably the standing stone, on the market place at Izier in 1586.

The Druids Hill of Marche-en-Famenne

Marche-en-Famenne 6900, Rue Cornimont
50°13'14.17"N – 5°20'8.24"E

The city of Marche-en-Famenne is also called the gateway to the Ardennes. That it was inhabited in the Stone Age was proven by the hundreds of stone spearheads that were found in the caves' Fond des Vaulx', east of the city.

West of Marche on the edge of town, a large lane laid out in the late 16th century and bordered with lime trees leads to the chapel of the Holy Trinity and a number of strange monuments. Some of these trees would be 275 years old. Beech trees and oaks are also present, of which some are over 350 years of age, and some fifteen other species are to be discovered. The woods and paths scattered with benches are an invitation to a stroll in this peaceful area.

A large flat rock is traditionally considered as a Druids Altar, but also used by the Old Germanic tribes as an altar for Odin. Maybe this is the reason

The Druids Altar or Calvary and the mausoleum.

why the site was Christianized in the early 7th century. First a hermit lived on the hill, later a chapel was built on the place of the old hermitage. The original Chapel of the Holy-Trinity is gone but a new one was built in 1515. However, a stone dating from the year 1305 was included in the south wall. It is probably one of the older stone chapel, of which the foundations have been recovered. The seven Stations of the Cross were added in 1642 all along the alley of lime trees. The new hermitage was built in 1975.

In the rocks near the Druids Altar is a small natural cave which strangely enough is called 'Le Tombeau' (the tomb). This strange tomb is compared, sometimes identified, as the tomb of Christ. The distance from there to the centre of Marche-en-Famenne is assumed to be equal to the distance from Christ's Tomb in Palestine to the city of Jerusalem.

Until 1667 it was possible to visit the cave in its natural state. In 1715, a mausoleum was built under the overhanging rock next to the cave. A crucifix was placed on the Druid altar and since then the rock was called the Calvary Mountain.

On this holy hill, known as 'Le Monument' several miraculous healings took place according to the legend, even during the last three centuries. There were even brought stillborn children and it was also an important station for the pilgrims, coming from the east and north to the famous shrine of Santiago de Compostela in Spain.

Spa: the footprint of Saint Remacle

Spa 4900, Chemin des Fontaines
50°29'6.71"N – 5°53'52.08"E

The Holy Remacle visited the Ardennes in the 7th century to purge the region of paganism and spread Christianity. Apparently, he fulfilled his role very well because after his missionary work, he became Bishop of Maastricht and was canonized after his death. He is said to have stayed for years in a cave near the Semois in the village of Cugnon. An ancient cult site in the form of a Celtic oppidum and a Roman settlement was situated there. The place is still known as the 'Chateau du Fees' or the Castle of the Fairies.

Remacle left this place after some time and subsequently moved to Spa where he stayed at the source 'The Sauvinière', one of the oldest springs in Wallonia.

A rustic shelter protects the source and the imprint.

Next to the source is a strange stone bearing the imprint of a human foot. According to the legend, this was left by Remacle when he was Christianized the pagan source.

In the past, the pilgrims came to the source on September 3rd, the holiday of the saint, and filled the imprint with coins. This particular place was well known in the area for centuries due to a strange fertility ritual. Women who wished to become pregnant put their feet in the imprint and subsequently drunk nine beakers of water from the source.

If this operation was repeated for nine consecutive days at the same time, they would become pregnant within nine months and bear a healthy child. If their right foot was placed in the print they would give birth to a boy, the left foot guaranteed a girl.

This fertility ritual involves much more than superstition. In a period during which the number of miscarriages and stillborn children was very high, each method that could ensure a healthy child was welcome. The high iron content of the water must have helped those suffering from anemia, and increased the chances of conception of the future mother. Therefore Saint Remacle was also called upon to ensure a fruitful marriage.

According to archaeologists from the University of Liege, the footprint was made in prehistoric times. This means that this place has been sacred long before the region was Christianized. In the woods behind the well, there is an old stone called 'the Druid Stone'. It is a block of stone that has a kind of hole on one side. Rainwater that remains in this cavity is said to have healing powers.

Remacle with his wolf and his cave in Cugnon where he has stayed for many years.

On the other side of the well is the 'Bois de la Grosse Pierre' or 'Forest of the big stone'. The large stone which gives his name to the forest is gone, but bearing in mind the mission which Remacle fulfilled, we may assume that it was a megalith.

When Remacle met the Merovingian king Siegebert II in 645 he asked him to build two Monasteries in the Ardennes. When he was allowed to choose the places himself, he immediately picked two pagan shrines. His first choice was a Celtic cult place with springs. The monastery founded there was called Malmumdarium, which became the present city of Malmedy. The second monastery was named Stabulum, later known as Stavelot.

Remacle is always depicted with a wolf wearing a basket of building blocks. The Apostle of the Ardennes, as he is called, is said to have driven all the wolves out of the Ardennes after he had mastered the wolf that had bitten his donkey to death. Remacle has laid his pilgrim's staff on the back of the wolf, and commanded it to carry his burden for the rest of his life. The wolf instantly obeyed and remained in the animal pack of the saint. The shrine containing some of the bones of Remacle can be visited in the Saint Sebastian's Church of Stavelot.

The Abbey of Orval

Villers-devant-Orval 6823, N 840
49°38'19.85"N – 5°20'53.79"E

The Abbey of Orval is one of the most remarkable Cistercian abbeys in Belgium. It is located in Villers-devant-Orval, in the in the Gaume region of Luxembourg. Set in a deep valley, it is still home to a bustling community of monks.

The abbey was founded in 1132, though there was already a chapel in the early 11th century. A group of Benedictine monks from Calabria settled there and started the construction of a church and monastery in 1070. For unknown reasons, they left after about 40 years and the construction work came to a halt.

Later a community of Canons built a new church which was consecrated in 1124. A few years later, in 1132, a group of Cistercian monks who had been sent by Saint Bernard from the Abbey of Trois-Fontaines in Champagne, came here and joined them to form a community within the Cistercian Order. The Cistercians purchased agricultural land and forests to be able to live according to the rules of the Holy Benedict; 'ora et labora' – pray and work.

In the second half of the 12th century, the building of a new bigger church was started and it was finished early in the 13th century. Unfortunately, the newly built cloister was destroyed by fire in 1252. It was reconstructed and extended during the 14th century, but during the 15th and 16th centuries, the wars between France and Burgundy and later between France and Spain brought havoc and devastation throughout the Luxembourg region and Orval was not spared.

While the 17th Century seems to be one of disaster for the Low Countries, Orval was to be at the highest point of its development. With the support of the Archduke Albert and Isabelle the monks started the building of a new neoclassical abbey next to the old. At the beginning of the 18th century, the abbey counted 130 monks, 90 choristers and 40 lay brothers. However, in 1793, both monasteries were again destroyed by the French revolutionaries.

The 17 meter high statue on the new church and the miraculous well.

The building of the new abbey started in 1928, the church tower was finished in 1931 and the basilica was completed in 1936. In 1948, all of the buildings were finished and the church was solemnly consecrated on September 8. Today's community consists of about 20 monks including novices and professed.

As soon as you enter the abbey, you are struck by the beauty of the view on the guest quarters while further up on the gable of the church, an extraordinary statue of Our Lady with the Christ Child catches the visitor's eyes. Our Lady has a long straight nose and wears a curious hat that looks very Egyptian. Also Jesus is shown in a very strange way as a young boy with curly hair. The statue is 17 metres high and weighs 22 tons. The setting in the valley is quite superb and attributes to a feeling of majesty and peace. The natural setting, the warmth of the yellow stones and the quiet beauty of the ruins are beautiful.

According to legend; Countess Mathilde of Tuscany founded the abbey in the 11th century, and she – as well as the abbey itself – are shrouded in mystery. The wedding ring of Mathilde had accidentally fallen into a well. She prayed to the Lord and suddenly a trout rose to the surface with the ring in its mouth. 'This truly is a Valley of Gold!' Mathilde exclaimed and out of gratitude, she built the abbey of the Golden Valley, the Val d'Or, Orval.

The miraculous 'Wishing Well' still exists; if you throw a coin in the water, you may make a wish. To this day, Orval beer is made with water from that very same spring which supplies water to the monastery and its brewery. The abbey arms show the trout and ring and the famous trout became also the beer's label.

Also the great the French prophet, Michel de Nostradame is said to have stayed for a while in Orval were he received his visions under the big oak tree. He wrote there some quatrains that undoubtedly could be interpreted as talking about a treasure in Orval.

Quatrain 27, Century 1:
Beneath the oak tree, struck by lightning,
Not far from there the treasure is hidden,
Which has been gathered for many centuries.
When found, a man shall die by a spring, the eye pierced.

Did he speak about the treasure of the Merovingian King Dagobert II who was killed in the Forest of Woevres near Stenay in France, some 25 kilometres southwest of Orval? Dagobert II was murdered near a well, where his left eye was pierced by a lance. However, a treasure is never found.

Is this the oak where Nostradame was talking about?

Different ley lines run through many places in the abbey ruins but not trough the new abbey buildings. Clearly, it seems the knowledge was lost a long time ago. You can find them as usual in the abbey church near the High Altar, near the famous oak and by the well.

Although the new abbey cannot be visited, the services, which are sung in French, are accessible to everyone who wishes to join the monks' payers (mass on Sundays at 9:30, and Saturdays at 11:30).

Province Hainaut

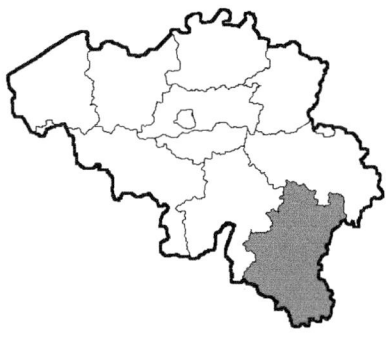

Hollain, Pierre Brunehaut

Hollain 7620, Rue des six Chemins
50°31'33.75"N – 3°24'56.77"E

In Hollain we find the largest standing stone of Belgium. It is 4.40 meters high, three meters wide, weighs over thirty tons and is believed to be rooted three meters into the ground. It gets his name because it can easily be reached by the Chemin d' Hollain, an old Roman road that runs from Bavay to Cassel. The track was named after Brunehilde, a Frankish queen from the 6th century.

When Clotherius II conquered her country, she was not only captured, but also had to undergo several humiliations. She was tied naked onto a horse and chased into the army camp where she was laughed at and beaten. After three days of suffering Brunhilde died while she was still tied onto the horse. The standing stone is said to remember that place.

But like most megaliths, this stone also bears reference to different legends. According to one story, the stone was wanted very much for the construction of the Cathedral of Tournai. As the transportation was stopped during the night, the next morning the labourers discovered that the stone had disappeared. Later it became clear that it had returned to its original position.

The notch that can be seen in the middle of the stone has, using a little imagination, the shape of a footprint. A legend tells that this is likely caused by the Holy Virgin who had ordered the used the stone to build the cathedral. When she noticed that other stones were used, she rose from the stone back to heaven and left her footprint behind. Tradition tells that if the stone would fall over, the end of the world would be near.

The Pierre Brunehaut has a slanted top, so it may have been used for astronomical observations. It is in a north-south orientation with the top corner facing north. This means that it was placed deliberately towards the constellation Ursa Major if you use the sloping side as a visor. A large number of standing stones in Wallonia have a slanted top so it looks like they show at some point in the sky.

Apart from this stone we could find another one in Gozée, Estines au Val and Rièzes in the province of Hainaut, in Neerwinden in Flemish Brabant and Chaumont-Gistoux and Thorambais-Saint-Trond in Walloon Brabant. However, those Belgian menhirs are not unique and they do not all point at the same direction. We can also find them in other countries. The best known group of this type are the 'Stones of Stennes' on the Orkney Islands, north of Scotland.

Old illustration of the torture of Brunehilde.

The large standing stone.

Bibliography

Balau S., Les sources de l'histoire de Liège au Moyen Age, Uitg. Bruxelles, Lamertin 1903
Bransly E.: Revue internationale de radiesthésie, Bruxelles, 1946
Brou W. & M.: Nos pierres et leurs legendes, Techniques et scientifiques, Bruxelles, 1979
Brou W. & M.: Le secret des druides, Bruxelles, 1970
Claes J. & A. & Vincke K.: geneesheiligen in de Lage Landen, Davidsfonds Leuven, 2005
Clerinx H.: Kathedralen uit de steentijd, Davidsfonds Leuven, 2001
Comblin J. C.: Wéris en histoire, contes et légendes du pays de Durbuy, 1980
Danthine H.: Un menhir découvert à Weris en 1947, anales de l'institut archéologique du Luxembourg, nr 92, 1961
Davidson J.: Radiation; What it is, What it does to us & What we can do about it, C. W. Daniel, 1986
Davidson H.R. Ellis: Myths and symbols in Pagan Europe, Manchester Univ. Press, 1988
De Cock A.: Volksgeneeskunde in Vlaanderen, Gent, 1891
De Jong N.: Esoterisch christendom, Rune, 1999
Devereux P.: Earth memory, Quantum, 1991
Evans J.: Mind, body and Elctromagnetism, Element, 1986
Farwerck F. E.: De mysteriën der oudheid en hun inwijdingsriten, Hilversum
Gheraert Lienhout; natuurkunde van het geheelal, Oudenaarde, stadsarchief.
Geysen C.: Abdij van Sint-Bernaerts, Gemeentebestuur Boechout, 1996
Gids voor Vlaanderen, toeristische en culturele gids van de Vlaamse gemeenten, Lannoo, 1995
Giraldo W.: Duizend jaar mirakels in Vlaanderen, uitgeverij Van de Wiele, Brugge 1995
Giraldo W.: Volksdevotie in West Vlaanderen, uitgeverij Van de Wiele, Brugge 1989
Gramaye: 1610 Antverpensiae Antiquitates, Brussel
Harroy E.: Cromlechs & dolmens de Belgique, 1889
Harsema O. H.: Geschiedenis in het landschap, Assen, 1990
Hendriks J.: Archeologie in de Lage Landen, Prisma, 1994
Heuvel H. W.: Volksgeloof en Volksleven, Zutphen, 1909
Hitching F.: De megalietenbouwers, Amsterdam boek b.v., 1976
Jacques F.: Saint Mort, sa vie, ses reliques, son pelgrinage, Editions Condroz-Meuze-Haillot, 1971
Jarricot J.: La radiesthésie, Paris, 1959

Jöckle Clemens: Heiligen van alle Tijden, uitgeverij Verba, 2003
Jongen L.: Heiligenlevens in Nederland en Vlaanderen, Bert Bakker, Amsterdam, 1998
Kiesel F.: Légendes des Quatre Ardennes, 1977
Lambrechts M.: Bezem en Kruis. Grepen uit het Zuidkempische volksgeloof, Retie, 1974
Lampen: Willibrord en Bonifacius, Amsterdam, 1939
Lindemans J.: Toponymische verschijnselen, Standaard Brussel, 1954
Mc Kenna T. & Mc Kenna D.: The invisible landscape: Mind, hallucinogens, and the I Ching. Harper, San Francisco, 1993
Metha A. K.: Genezen met magneten, Ankh-Hermes, 1987
Michell J.: Megalithomania, Thames and Hudson, London, 1982
Michell J.: The earth spirith, Thames and Hudson, London, 1975
Pattie F. A.: Mesmer and Animal Magnetism; A Chapter in the History of Medicine, Edmonston Publishing, 1994
Peeters K. C.: Eigen Aard. Grepen uit de Vlaamse folklore, Antwerpen, 1946
Pellaert T. & Geentjens E.: Magie, hekserij en volksgeloof, Pelckmans, 1986
Persinger M.: Space-time transients, Nelson-Hall, 1977
Pohl, G. von: Erdstrahlen als Krankheitserregen, München, 1932
Prims F.: Geschiedenis van Antwerpen, deel 1-2-9-16, Standaard Brussel 1927
Presman A. S.: Electromagnetic fields and life, Plenum, 1970
Purner J.: Radiästhesie, Ein Weg zum Licht? M&T Zürich, 1988
Saint-Hilaire P. de: De geneesheiligen, Brussel, 1991
Saint-Hilaire P. de: Raadselachtige Ardennen, Brussel, 1976
Saint-Hilaire P. de: Raadselachtig België, Brussel, 1973
Schelfhout Frans: Lief Millegem, uitgeven door de millegemvrienden, 1983
Sirjacobs Raymond: Sint-Pauluskerk – Historische gids, vzw Sint-Paulusvrienden
Top S.: Volksverhalen uit Vlaams Brabant, Het Spectrum, Utrecht, 1982
Valgaerts E. & Machiels L.: De Keltische erfenis: Riten en symbolen in het volksgeloof, Stichting Mens en cultuur, Gent, 1992
Van Biervliet A. t.: Heiligen uit ons volk, Brugge, 1987
Van Cauwenbergh G.: Gids voor Antwerpen, tussen Leien en Singel, Hadewijch, 1988
Van Caukerken L: Cronijcke der stadt Antwerpen
Van Coppenolle M.: Uitvaartgebruiken in West Vlaanderen, Volkskunde jaargang 1951, nr 3
Van Dale: Etymologisch woordenboek, Van Dale lexicografie, BV Utrecht 1993
Van den Berg: Volksverhalen uit Antwerpen, Het Spectrum, Utrecht, 1981
Wouters van Weerden A.: Tussen Wodan en Widar, Vrij Geestesleven, 1997

Index

Abbey of Herkenrode 83, 84
Albert and Isabella of Austria 71, 72
Alfred Watkins 9, 60
Andenne 89, 90
Animism 15
Anne Bertrand 98
Anselmo Adornes 29
Antwerp 51

Barvaux 93
Basilica of Scherpenheuvel 69
Becquerel 10
Bernard of Clervaux 87
Black Madonna 76, 77, 89
Book of Revalation 15
Bruges 25, 26, 29, 43,
Brunehilde 107
Brussels 56, 72, 74

Chapel of Saint Mort 91
Chapel of the Green Hill 68
Chapel of the Holy Trinity 99
Chartres 77
Church of Saint Andreas 54
Church of Saint Catharina 55
Cistercian order 103
Cross Chapel 41
Crow chapel 36
Cugnon 100

Dagobert II 105
Denderwindeke 49

Devil's Stone 90, 91, 102
Devils Bed 96
dowsing 12, 13
dragons 76
Druids Altar 99, 100
Duke John of Brabant 83

Eksaarde 40
electromagnetic radiation 48
Emblem 61, 65
ex voto's 27, 40

Fault lines 8, 9, 56, 58, 63
Fountain of the Five Wounds 73

Gamma rays 10
Gaverland 40
Geel 66
Geiger counter 10
Geraardsbergen 43
Germanics 43, 76, 79, 99
Gistel 33-35
Goddess Hella 78
Godelieve from Gistel 33
green man 21, 22
Grimde 78, 79, 80

Haillot 89
Hakendover 78, 79, 80
Halle 44, 75, 77
Helene Danthine 94
Hemiksem 56

Herstappe 82
Hildegard von Bingen 15
Hollain 107
Holly Begga 90
Holy Benedict 88, 103
Holy Blood relic 27
Holy Dimpna 66
Holy Dimpna Chapel 68
Holy Evermarus 81
Holy Gummarus 61, 64
Holy Lambert 49
Holy Remacle 100
Holy Sepulchre 30
Holy Well 42
Hotton 95
Hove 59, 61
Huy 90

Izier 98

Jeruzalem Church 29, 32

Kuringen 83

Laken 71
Leonie Van den Dyck 46
Ley lines 9, 10, 13, 32, 45, 48, 53, 54, 56, 60, 71, 73, 83, 85, 97, 105
Lier 61, 62
Lit du Diable 96
Lourdes 11, 46

Malmedy 103
Marche-en- Famenne 99
Mariette Beco 46
Mathilde of Tuscany 104
Medjugorje 48
Melsele 39
Michel de Nostradame 104
Millegem, Ranst 59

Morville 98

Odin 99
Onkerzele 45, 46, 48
Oppagne 94, 98
Orval 103, 104
Oudeberg 43
Our Lady's Cathedral 51
Our Lady of Gaverland 40
Our Lady of the Old Mountain 43
Our Lady of the Stone Chapel 79
Ozo 98

Pagan 43
Persinger Michaël 11
Pierra Haina 96
Pierre Brunehaut 107

Radiation 9, 10
Rutten 81, 83

Sacred Meadow 81, 82
Saint Anne 73
Saint Bernard 56, 103
Saint Catharina 29, 55
Saint George 22, 63, 64
Saint John 60
Saint Lambert's Chapel 49
Saint Martin 75
Saint Maurus 80
Saint Michaël 22, 57
Saint Michael's Cathedral 74
Saint Mort 89, 90
Saint Paulus Church 56
Saint Pieter's Chapel 63, 66
Saint Walburgis Church 97
Saint Winoksbergen 35
Santiago de Compostela 81, 100
Schelle 51, 56
Scherpenheuvel 69

Serotonine hormone 11
solstice line 59
Spa 100
Stavelot 103
Stenay 105
Stonehenge 11, 85

Tienen 80
Tongeren 82

unicorn 83, 84

Villers-devant-Orval 105
Villers-la-Ville 56, 84, 87
Vremde 59, 60

Walpurga 96
Werbomont 98
Weris 93, 96, 97
Wodan 76

Zammel 68
Zonhoven 85